Super ADHD

ADHD Hope and Help
from Real, Successful People with
ADHD

RACHEL KNIGHT

Copyright © 2017 Clare Jackson

All rights reserved.

ISBN: 1976408466
ISBN-13: 978-1976408465

DEDICATION

This book is dedicated to my favourite past employer, Liz, who filled me with awe when she interviewed me, and hasn't stopped to this day. Spending time with her gave me the rarest of buzzes, that can only come from people who see the world through an exciting and colourful lens. A testament to the blessings of ADHD, her visionary entrepreneurialism and ability to "charm the pants off people" made her a trail blazer in her industry. And besides all of that, she's a darn-tootin' cool lady.

CONTENTS

ACKNOWLEDGMENTS	**6**
INTRODUCTION	**8**
WHAT IS ADHD?	**13**
REAL-LIFE ADHD SUPERSTARS	**16**
Kyle Goodwin	18
"Doctor Mo"	30
Kat Wczesniak	55
Alex H.	65
Ray Weer	71
Veronica Roan	78
"Liz"	83
ARE THERE POSITIVE SIDES TO ADHD?	**85**
The Gift of Hyper-Focus	86
The Gift of Energy and Excitement	88
The Gift of Independent Thought	90
The Gift of Bravery	93
The Gift of Tenacity and Drive	95
CAN ADHD BE HARNESSED?	**98**
Finding and Channelling Passions	98
Passions of the Superstars	101
HOW DID ADHD AFFECT SCHOOL?	**103**
Alternative Schooling Systems	105
Challenges: Force, Punishment, Rebellion and Boredom	107
Challenges: Dropping out of School or University	112
A Flexible Approach to Learning	116
HOW DID ADHD AFFECT FAMILY LIFE?	**120**
Framing ADHD Correctly	121
Did family approaches to learning affect them?	122
Challenges: Rebellion Against Parents	124
Parents as inspiration	128
Did their families worry?	130
CAREER AND LIFESTYLE CHOICES	**134**
Why do they lead unusual lives?	134

What made them start their own businesses?	**142**
Challenges: Expectations, Problems Fitting-In and Shame	**144**
REFERENCES	**149**
APPENDICES	**151**
Example Games for ADHD Kids to Find their Gifts	**151**
ABOUT THE AUTHOR	**159**
BOOKS BY RACHEL KNIGHT	**160**
SIGN UP TO THE READING LIST	**161**

ACKNOWLEDGMENTS

I would like to thank all my ADHD-gifted friends, for always being interesting, never failing to surprise me, and choosing inspirational lifestyles to emulate. My friend Kat who created a business model from her bucket list, Alex who trades in gold, silver and oil, doctor Mo who saves lives and conquered the Middle East with his nutrition company, and Kyle who somehow manages to do the work of an entire army with one pair of hands. Without your examples, I might be forgiven for believing the widely held story about ADHD, that the negatives outweigh the positives. But looking more closely, I realised the *only* successful entrepreneurs that I personally know, *all* have ADHD. And they *all* have interesting lives.

Introduction

ADHD seems to be everywhere. Controversy surrounds it. Stories of disruption, drug abuse, imprisonment, and lives lived in chaos abound. As an adult who has ADHD, a teenager growing up thinking about what the future holds, or a parent of a child with ADHD, you might be forgiven for worrying. You might be forgiven for saying "I might as well not try." ADHD means x, y and z, and destiny is already pre-written. What an incredible stigma to face. This book is written to tell you, in a highly unscientific and un-politically correct way, that such a conclusion is a load of old cr*p. I decided to write this book when an interesting thought struck me:

Every successful entrepreneur in my phonebook has ADHD.

How could this be? Wasn't ADHD meant to be a bad thing? How could it be that the most vivacious people I know seem to be thriving when they are meant to have a disorder? In comparison to many of my non-ADHD contacts, the ADHD'ers positively shine as beacons of inspiration. Everywhere they go they're greeted with wonder at how they manage to achieve so much, or how they're living such exciting lives. At the risk of offending the rest of my friends and colleagues, they're the most engaging bunch I can imagine. There would be no hesitation if my fairy godmother asked me what kind of life I would prefer to lead, if I could pick between the two groups (ADHD'ers or non-ADHD'ers). I'm sure I'll be disowned for this comment.

To satisfy my curiosity about what was going on, I decided to interview them, and publish their thoughts in this book, to see what lessons could be learnt.

Why did they lead such unusual lives? What made them start their own businesses or work for themselves? How has ADHD affected them? And how did they find their passions?

As medical doctor and entrepreneur, Mo- who has moderate inattentive ADHD- explained, a normal person "who has no technical or specific knowledge of ADHD, who has been hearing about it in the media, is going to look at it as a disease. Which in many situations it is, but they won't see the positive aspects of it, because that's not the side that's advertised."

What are these positive sides? Can they be harnessed?

One thing became abundantly clear during the interviews. These people, my friends, have passion for what they do oozing from their pores. Perhaps not everyone, in everything that they do, but when it comes to their areas of interest, they had me drawn in, hooked, and carried away with their enthusiasm.

I can't help but wonder if these are typical ADHD'ers, or some kind of atypical, super-human subgroup. The truth is, that question can never be answered. As anecdotal evidence, there can be no statistical conclusions drawn about whether this sample is representative of a wider population. But even if it's not representative of the ADHD community as-a-whole, I love the way that my friends are a living rebellion against the accepted "norm." The idea that ADHD is some kind of terrible affliction, or a sentence that will ruin your life, in their cases, is simply not true. For them, despite the challenges and difficulties being faced- particularly during their school years and early careers- the outcome has been quite the opposite. The strengths of ADHD have left them at a positive advantage over much of the population, in terms of pursuing their own goals and living life unashamedly on their own terms.

The interviews focus on four main areas, to try and help crystallize some insights, straight for the horses' mouths:

- Identifying passions
- Lessons and tips about schooling and parenting
- Career and lifestyle choices
- Challenges faced

We focus on how our superstars have found inspiration, identified passions and channelled these for success. Their chosen lifestyles work *with* the ADHD brain, harnessing its vigilance for interesting, dopamine-inducing activities. They have allowed their addictive tendencies to fall on pursuits that were productive and made them happy.

This book is a metaphorical protest *against* the abundant literature that discusses almost all aspects of ADHD as "problems." It focuses instead on how to look at the flip side of the coin and celebrates how people with ADHD creatively forge their own paths.

This positive approach is favoured over the task of how to make an ADHD'er fit into the glove of a "normal" life. Or how to help them do their homework, not answer back or pay their bills on time (there is enough material written on surmounting these challenges). In fact, we learn how some of our interviewees have avoided a situation where they were forced into a shoe that didn't fit, and in breaking free re-discovered their unique identity.

That said, this is not a thesis, research study or statistical summary of evidence on ADHD. It doesn't intend to tell you what to think, or get involved in the politics of whether to medicate, whether to call ADHD a superpower, learning disability or a disorder. It's simply some anecdotal inspiration to highlight how there are two sides to this story. In the words of doctor Mo (and I'll be calling him that for the entirety of this book, don't you know):

> "When you're researching always stick to the facts. It's good to learn about things from different sources, [such as this book, for example] but it's very important to look at what the recent research says. It's good to keep an evidence-based approach."

Caveats aside, our ADHD superstars are unafraid, unabashed, and possess the tenacity to get things done. You'll see that the energy that is so common amongst ADHD'ers, is so often admired by others.

What is ADHD?

ADHD is short for attention deficit hyperactivity disorder. There are three main subtypes, hyperactive, inattentive or a combination of the two. Everyone's experience of ADHD is said to be slightly different, with various traits ranging from a lack of choice over what absorbs or repels your attention, impulsivity, hyperactivity, excitability, creativity, anxiety, sometimes lots of energy and sometimes a great imagination.

It's often discovered at school, when children must sit down and pay attention to lessons for long periods of time, or are required to do homework. This can be a challenge for children with ADHD if they are not interested in a subject, as their attention is likely to drift elsewhere, onto subjects or activities that they do find absorbing.

Hyperactive and combined types of ADHD are easier to spot, which is more common in boys than in girls, as when they become bored they tend to "fidget" or become disruptive or irritable. If this is coupled with impulsivity, behavioural problems may ensue. Inattentive children without the hyperactivity element are less likely to be discovered, as they are likely to quietly sit and daydream rather than draw attention to themselves. This type of ADHD is more common in girls than in boys, meaning it is more likely for girls to slip under the radar and not get the guidance they need.

In terms of fitting into society's expectations of orderliness, calmness, organisation, sociability, romance and a nine to five job; these elements may or may not be possible for a lot of ADHD'ers, even if they attempt to conform (although many choose not to). The consequences can create huge challenges for many people and parents.

Drug and alcohol abuse have been strongly connected with ADHD in several studies. One study found that in the U.S. 25% of adults being treated for alcohol and substance abuse have ADHD. Another study found that at age 15, 40% of children with ADHD had started drinking alcohol, compared with 22% of children without ADHD- a strong predictor of substance and alcohol abuse in adulthood.[5]

Looking at the prison population, 21-45% of those incarcerated have ADHD, as shown in 15 studies from peer reviewed journals. People with ADHD are 4 to 9 times more likely to commit crimes and go to jail than their non-ADHD counterparts. [6]

I would be looking through extremely rose-tinted glasses if I pretended that everyone with ADHD has got an incredible opportunity to harness an inner passion and transform the world in some way. But are there things that can be learnt from our successful ADHD superstars? By understanding the world through their eyes can we help more people make ADHD an advantage and avoid dropping out of the system?

Real-Life ADHD Superstars

As you know, all of the ADHD superstars that I have interviewed come from my burgeoning phonebook. As such, I love them all, and am incredibly biased on their behalf. My friends are not unreachable oligarchs, they're aspirational but real people, leading successful lives. I decided to interview them on their experiences after it struck me that there was a mismatch between the expectation of ADHD being a bad thing, and the fact that amongst the people I know, it seems to lead to entrepreneurial and lifestyle success.

On further investigation, it was unsurprising to find that people with ADHD are 300% more likely to start their own businesses. Colossally successful entrepreneurs Sir Richard Branson (Founder of Virgin and Adventurer), Ingvar Kamprad (Founder of Ikea) and David Neeleman (Founder of JetBlue) all attribute their achievements to be partially *because* of their ADHD, rather than despite it.[1]

But it doesn't stop at entrepreneurialism. Gold-medal-winning Olympic swimmer Michael Phelps channelled his energy into training, racking up 14 golds at the Athens and Beijing Olympics. Emma Watson was diagnosed as a child and after finding fame on screen has found passion to tirelessly advocate women's rights around the globe. Grammy-winning musician Justin Timberlake reports himself to have ADD and OCD. This may be one reason he has the energy and drive to not only be a singer-songwriter but a restaurateur, tequila distiller, NBA part-owner, record executive and clothier.[2-4] When an ADHD'er finds their sweet-spot, it seems like magic can happen.

In fact, it appears that they can do *anything that captures their interest*.

Kyle Goodwin

Founder of Drafted magazine (augmented reality print/digital publication) and Click Content (content agency), plays in two bands

Industry: Journalism, digital content strategy and creation, musician

Age: 31

ADHD Type: Combined, childhood diagnosis, unknown severity

First up is seemingly super-human Kyle Goodwin, founder of Drafted magazine- an augmented reality print/digital publication, and Click Content- a digital content agency. Kyle has channelled his boundless energy into doing the work of a small army, working seventeen-hour days if needed, without feeling the heat.

Equally at home in high-end suits as he is in outrageously cool hooded sweaters and pumps, he sports a shock of spikey black hair, thick stubble, and a slightly mad look in his eyes. When Kyle fixes you in his laser beam, there's no mistaking you're being hyper-focused on. This bad-boy-gone-good was kicked out of school for rebelling against the machine, and taught himself everything he needed to know to have a successful career in journalism and business.

He'll bamboozle you with his sales-pitch, infect you with his enthusiasm, and shock you with his f-bombs, but still you'll take him home to grandma, and trust him with the key to your safety deposit box. Instinctively you know, he's one of the most decent people you could hope to meet.

When he's not working, he's playing in two bands (yes, *two* bands), or socialising until the early hours of the morning. Ladies, prepare to blush. Gentlemen, prepare to be impressed. I give you, the unabashed force that is *Mister Kyle Goodwin*...

Tell me about your experience of ADHD.

From my experience, what I've found is that ADHD can be a gift, but only if you really master how to channel it. Back in school, it's a hindrance. Because if something doesn't grab your attention or light a bit of a fire in you, from my perspective, I just didn't give a sh*t. Couldn't focus on it. But not just that, I became kind of very disruptive around it.

But, the moment that I found something that deeply excited me, I could channel that energy. And be able to do things that a lot of the people around me weren't able to achieve. And I'd go so far above and beyond. I carried that attitude and ethic into my professional life. The energy that you can create around your passions is endless.

Can you tell me about your first business?

I started my first company in 2012, called Drafted magazine. We used augmented reality technology to link print and digital media platforms.

It was very new at the time, 80% of our print magazine was digitally interactive. We'd interview a celebrity, like Keira Knightly, film some exclusive video content, and the only way you could actually access that was by scanning your phone over a specific page in the magazine using an augmented reality app. It opened all these doors to advertisers that had never been possible before.

I had the idea with a mate of mine … about how this could be the future of media. We said, "imagine what you can do with that."

So, would you say impulsivity, which is a characteristic of ADHD, helps when you have an idea?

Yes. I handed in my notice for my job the next day. Put a business model together for this. We went out and started pitching for investment, and we got £50,000. It's nothing in that industry. Our primary competitors were Stylist and Shortlist magazine who started with £4,000,000 of investment. So, you could see what we were up against.

Initially I was doing four or five full time jobs, just on my own. So, I was writing about 80% of the magazine. I was doing the stylistic specs and design. I was overseeing the sales and commercial side, the print and distribution runs. The logistics were wildly mind-blowing. I was working seventeen, eighteen-hour days, every day, for the first four months. But without ever feeling tired, without ever feeling run down or close to a break down. And under extreme pressure as well. I just went with it.

Did you always know what you were interested in, or did you struggle to find the right path at any point?

Yeah. In my early years, I got kicked out of school before my GCSEs. I got in a lot of trouble, I was extremely disruptive. I couldn't abide by the school system, I couldn't play by the rules. `I had to ask why. Everything was "Why do I need to tuck my shirt in?" "Why can't I listen to music on my lunchbreak?" Questioning everything. Obviously, the school system doesn't want you to do that, the school system wants you to just say "yes sir, no sir" and do as you're **** told. It breeds a level of conformity. And I was never just that person.

After that I was a musician for many years. I toured a lot with my bands. Partying a lot, meeting lots of people, building up my social skills. It wasn't until I got into journalism that I had a professional goal to channel my energy into. I still play in two different bands, and I still find time to fit that in.

That's definitely going into your summary. "Plays in two bands."

So, do you have a problem being employed, having a boss or a manager?

No. I don't think I do. I don't think I have a problem answering to people, it just depends on their attitude and tone. I have to work within a collaborative environment. I can't work within a totalitarian environment at all. That I would rebel against immediately, no matter what the circumstances. But even now, I have a bunch of clients, and we're very much working together on projects. They have the power to keep me on or not, but it's a collaborative process.

And you're the expert I guess?

Exactly. I'm the authority. I have a lot of leeway and a lot of room to create and drive projects forward within my vision.

In my early days in journalism, I worked for very rowdy titles. I worked for Vice magazine, all my early features were just mental. My first series for them I pitched an idea where I would go to a global food chain, like Starbucks and McDonalds, actually get a job, go through the training, and then on my first day try to get fired as quickly as I could, and writing about my experiences doing it. I got sacked in 52 minutes.

Most people who don't have ADHD, would have an insane idea, and would never do anything with them. I actually went and did them. Looking back, it's an insane thing to do. The article is still up, you can still read them to this day.

I did loads of training to keep a straight face. I'd go into a posh Italian restaurant with my mate and order bolognaise, and then talk loudly about politics and sociology, whilst literally not using our hands. Just putting our face into our plate. Invariably the manager would come over and we'd – purely as training to keep a straight face- we'd tell this manager with sauce all over my face that we were members of a new religion called Apeanity, and we didn't believe in using knives and forks because it defied our animalistic heritage.

The amount of people that would say "Kyle, this is mental, what are you doing!?" but nothing would have stopped me from going through with that idea.

ADHD is about grabbing hold of an idea that you're excited about, and channelling all your energy into that. And it's amazing what you can achieve. Nothing could have stopped me doing [my ideas].

That's my little soundbite for how being headstrong and rebellious can also be seen as tenacious and driven.

You come across as incredibly positive in general.

Yeah. Yeah, yeah, yeah, yeah, yeah. * I acknowledge the choices I have at different moments, where I could potentially get worried, or anxious or scared of something. I'm very good at being able to acknowledge the choices I have, and being able to pick which one I want. It's about getting from A to B in the most simple, hassle-free way.

(*All "yeah"s included for tongue-in-cheek, humorous reasons.)

Can you tell me about your current company?

We're a content agency, so we work for a variety of brands, some large some small. And we create and manage digital content platforms and digital magazines for them.

Again, when I started this company, I was working seventeen hours a day. Going nuts. And even to this day I'm very hands on still. I have a lot of trouble delegating.

And why's that?

I feel like it's my baby. Whenever we have new proposals in or whenever we're launching a new platform, I'm there every day, there all night. And if anybody else has to work late I'm always there with them. The ADHD side really helps me with that. Particularly when I've had a long day and I'm under a lot of pressure and a lot of stress. I've been working for ten hours during the day, running around at meetings, pushed to my limit on so many levels, and then when all you really want to do is go home and watch a movie in your pants, I have to go to this little café near my house and work through my deadlines.

Well, *you* might want to watch movies in your pants.

I think without that level of ADHD driving and underpinning the energy that I'm putting into this, I'm not sure I'd have been able to achieve a lot of the things that I've done in my life.

Do you have any experience of parenting techniques, what works and what doesn't for you?

I got diagnosed with ADHD when I was very young. I was a rowdy kid. I was boisterous. I was ridiculous as well. I spent four months once when I was four refusing to wear my clothes the right way around. My mum had to put up with so much, you can just imagine, I was so boisterous. And she could have just shoved these pills in my face and shut me up, you know. But she didn't.

And she guided me through all of that, and my teenage years, when I was always getting into trouble at school. She always offered me love and support and always understood where I was coming from and tried to help and guide me. Instead of punishing me, she really nurtured me through that.

I can certainly vouch for the fact that my mum gave me a lot of freedom, and I'm a very confident and self-assured person these days. I don't know how much that has to do with it, but that's my experience.

But you never felt ashamed for having ADHD?

No quite the opposite, I was proud of it. I still am today, I am deeply proud of it. Haha. I recommend it to you.

You're like the poster boy of ADHD.

Any thoughts on the schooling system, in terms of what's good about it, what's needs to change about it?

Yeah, I certainly do… Knowledge and education are hugely important to me. I read a lot. I've read a lot of philosophy, classic literature, Russian literature from the eighteen-hundreds. It's very important for me to be a knowledgeable person in life.

But back in school, I hated it. I think where the school system fails us all is that they place far more emphasis on following the rules. And when I say rules I mean pointless stupid rules that are in no way necessary to a child's blossoming mind when it comes to education.

My teachers were genuinely more concerned with my shirt being tucked in than me actually getting a decent education. They couldn't acknowledge this. I would be disruptive in school, and no teacher would ever ask me, why. "Why did you behave like that in class, Kyle?" I would get punished. And that punishment would perpetuate into more disruptive behaviour. Because you can't punish a kid for the way that they're feeling about something without ever asking them why, and expect that to be the answer. Expect them to say "okay, lesson learned, I'm going to be a good boy now," it does not work like that.

But actually, if one of my teachers had sat me down and tried to explain to me, on a human level, why I had to tuck my shirt in, or why I wasn't allowed to listen to music on my lunchbreak, or all of these things that I had an issue with, I would have been a different story at school. But punishment doesn't work with kids with ADHD. It generates more of a will to be disruptive, and to continue that behaviour that got you punished in the first place, it simply doesn't work.

There's no infrastructure within the system to encourage individuality, it's not there to encourage creativity, it's almost pushing kids through this funnel, and if you're not careful as a child, you're going to come out the same as everybody f***ing else, right? And you're just going to be another f***ing workforce person to go out into the world and work nine to five and come home and watch television, and have dinner and then wake up and then go to work, come home, watch television. And you're never going to live your life.

As soon as I finished school, and I was in charge of my own education, [I became] a very knowledgeable person. I've been able to apply a lot of this knowledge to my everyday life, I can hold my own in a conversation with academics. Obviously, that was in me, but the school system failed me by not encouraging me to blossom and flourish while I was there.

What do you think about query-based learning for ADHD kids?

Well, with ADHD kids, it comes back to finding and acknowledging a passion, anything with that, the options are endless. You can just go to the very, very, very top. Being able to distinguish this at a young age, it's difficult.

I appreciate that perhaps as a fourteen-year-old, you aren't going to find your passion points just yet, but, there will be things with any kid that they are passionate about. I had this with English and literature when I was at school, and music. But instead of allowing those things to flourish, and still teach me the basics of science and religious studies, so I still have a broad range of knowledge still, I was treated like everybody else, but my brain worked differently to everybody else.

And then, when I acted differently from everybody else, then I got punished for it. And then it became this totally endlessly self-perpetuating thing that got worse and worse and deepened and deepened until I got kicked out of school. The school system failed in so many ways.

Since then I've gone on to do all sorts of things. Without any help from the school system. I've done it on my own accord, without any higher education at all.

This seems to be a common theme that I'm hearing, that the school system lets kids with ADHD down, and just cater towards everybody else.

What's next for you?

This is the beautiful thing. I don't know. I love my life. I'm enjoying it. I wake up every morning feeling super happy every day. I feel super fulfilled, professionally, socially and philosophically. I don't know if other people have this, but I thrive not knowing what's next. I thrive just living in the moment, doing the next project. And it always leads to something bigger, and more exciting. But I never know what's around the corner, and I love it.

One of my biggest fears in life is being settled to a point where I could tell you what's going to happen in the next six months of my life. I have no idea what's going to happen in my life. I could be living in New York in six months, I have no idea. Opportunities just keep arising, and I have no idea what's next. And I love it. What a way to live life.

"Doctor Mo"

Medical doctor, business cofounder, medical technologist

Industry: medicine, nutrition, medical technology

Age: 28

ADHD Type: Inattentive, adulthood diagnosis, moderate severity

Doctor Mo has a knowing smile and such an air of cool cattery you'd be forgiven for believing you're watching an episode of "House." This doctor saved a homeless patient's life, arguably because of his obstinate ADHD traits. Refusing to discharge the patient as expected by his superiors, he undoubtedly prevented his death when the patient went into respiratory arrest, six hours later.

Switching seamlessly between modes, doctor Mo will be knee-deep in complex medical jargon one minute, the next he's overcome with a child-like fascination for animals (he feeds his hamsters every morning by letting them lick humous from the end of his finger).

Identifying as a natural entrepreneur, he has a passion for spotting trends and opportunities that he can learn about quickly, in order to provide a solution.

Diagnosed with moderate inattentive ADHD during his fifth year of medical school, he believes that misunderstandings about ADHD abound. He considers high-achieving individuals such as himself at risk of being treated poorly in the workplace due to the label of ADHD. Keen to be judged by merit of the standard of care that he delivers as a doctor- the same standards as his non-ADHD peers- I ask him why he has chosen to keep his identity hidden.

Why do you want to remain anonymous?

An average person who has no technical or specific knowledge of ADHD, who has been hearing about it in the media, is going to look at it as a disease. Which in many situations it is, but they won't see the positive aspects of it, because that's not the side that's advertised. It's always the pharma side that says you need to take medication that is advertised.

Do you believe that ADHD is a gift sometimes?

I don't know if it's a gift, it depends where you end up. In today's schooling system, it's usually going to have a negative impact, but some people manage to find a way to use the positive side of ADHD to help them in life, I think.

How do you think that happens?

For me it was when I found out I had ADHD. I read more about it and I realized I should pursue the positive aspects and try to make them work for me. If I were to say the most important thing to do after a diagnosis would be to learn more about it.

What can parents do?

The best thing to do if you're a parent is to find the Connor Questionnaire which is the standard ADHD diagnosis test used to diagnose and stratify people. There are 40-50 questions, including trick questions to catch people who are trying to fake the symptoms. Then you are grouped into no ADHD, mild, moderate or severe, and then also into inattentive, hyperactive or combined type of ADHD.

ADHD is a bit like autism, in the respect that there's a spectrum, some people just get chronic boredom, some get anxiety, some can't sit still and some people do the opposite and get absorbed into something and they can't do anything else. As one psychiatrist put it ADHD is not necessarily the inability to focus, it can be the inability to shift your focus from one thing to something else. It's not a lack of attention, it's a lack of being able to control your attention. That's why people who tend to get their attention stuck on something productive tend to do very well.

So, for people with ADHD and parents of children with ADHD, does that mean they should find something they are passionate about that is "productive" to get their attention "stuck" to, rather than letting something arise casually that might be damaging?

That's exactly what mothers of children with ADHD don't realize. Because people with ADHD will never be able to do something or learn something that they don't like. Even if you keep pushing them there's no point. So, the best thing to do as a parent is to pick your battles and find something that your child will be interested in, and at least they can learn something instead of learning nothing.

Think of ADHD as a characteristic rather than saying that people with ADHD are all going to love the same things. Not everyone with ADHD is going to love to code [computer programs], or love horse riding, or playing sports, but they are all going to get obsessed with something.

Reading is great for finding out what you like. Instead of trying an endless list of activities you can give your child a book to read on a subject or sport, or set yourself a study incentive about an activity, and then decide if it's something that could spark an "obsession," and then try it in real life. But expect to have to incentivize yourself or your child to read if they don't like reading. People with ADHD are good at covering a large spectrum of different subjects very quickly and picking up on what will interest them.

What problems might people face, when trying to identify a productive "passion" for themselves or their ADHD child?

The problems mums will face is that they don't want their children to take risk. From a mother's point of view, of course she cares if their child has fun but their main concern is that they make it on their own, you become successful and you don't end up in trouble, in jail or on drugs.

So, when you come up with an idea, they're going to think you're insane sometimes. Some mothers will just want you to do the boring things in life like your maths homework, tidying your room, a job, and nothing else. A lot of mothers. A lot of mothers might make their children feel ashamed for being who they are.

Sometimes if you have a good idea that sounds amazing, a lot of mothers won't want you to take that risk and potentially ruin your life if it fails. They want you to do the easy thing, make money and get a job. And be around. Mothers are often built to minimize risks through evolution, whereas often dads are the opposite. Mothers have to try and remember how they were, when they were children.

What kind of activities do you find exciting?

For me I was always chasing what they call the "flow" state. I've been doing this my whole life.

That's when you're enjoying what you're doing because you have the skillset not to struggle with an activity and to do it well, but the activity is challenging enough to be engaging, without being so challenging that it's exhausting. Practicing medicine is a perfect example of how this can manifest. If you're a consultant doing the job of a junior doctor, you're over skilled and the job won't be challenging enough to engage you, you'll be below flow state. For a junior doctor to perform a consultant's role would be anxiety-provoking, and they wouldn't have the skillset so again- out of flow state. A good match is needed for any hobby or job to be stimulating. If you get your job and a hobby in which you have a flow state, you're fine in life. What else do you need?

What kind of activities do you find boring?

Manual tasks. Regular stuff that bores people with ADHD. Cleaning, repetitive tasks. Laundry. Ironing. Putting my shopping away. Going shopping. Cooking.

Have you ever been able to make a boring task enjoyable by daydreaming at the same time?

I've tried to do it, but I can't multitask. So, if I'm cleaning, there's no way I can use my brain for anything else. I've tried. It's unpredictable. I think sometimes these mundane tasks can bring you a lot of anxiety, and the way to get rid of anxiety is to not care. So, you end up making your ADHD symptoms worse.

Do you have any tips for dealing with ADHD children?

It's very important to look at the aspect of how to deal with children with ADHD. It can seem like everything they do, they're doing it on purpose or vindictively, but that is almost never the case. So, it's good to bear that in mind when you're dealing with them.

For example, if someone is not paying attention when you're talking, it's not because they think what you're saying is boring or they don't care about you, it's because they literally can't focus. And don't criticize them because they're very sensitive to criticism, most kids with ADHD, which can lead to a lot of personality disorders, anxiety or depression, in my opinion. Because they don't feel they're good enough, because they're not conforming.

The last thing you want is your child to feel like they're not good enough, while actually they can have some of the most amazing ideas that can change the world. It's a very ironic for a child to be stuck in that situation.

What about things that ADHD people don't want to, or can't make themselves do?

The best thing to do is to give yourself or your child an incentive. I didn't want to read a lot as a child, so my mother paid me for every book that I finished. I'm not necessarily advocating this kind of incentive, but I don't think there's anything wrong with it, because it worked for me. Now I only read about subjects I like, so I get obsessed and read a lot about a subject.

In terms of school, the only way I got through school every day was by playing football. I'd go in, wait for four hours just thinking about lunchtime. At lunchtime, I wouldn't eat I'd go and play football. So that was the highlight of my day. Then when football was done I would sit through four or five hours of school so I could go home and play PlayStation. My whole world revolved around that. I liked people but it was boring to socialize, I couldn't spend ten minutes talking to someone about their dog or their cat or whatever.

Without a diagnosis, you feel weird that everyone else can do all of these things except you. But if you have all of the knowledge, and someone tells you why you can't do things, not because you lack something compared with all of the other children who can do all of these mundane tasks, it's because your brain is wired in a way that is slightly different. You'll be able to become an artist, an athlete, a business person. Show your children the plus side of having all of these traits, because most kids can't see it yet, they're still so young. They get immersed in a world of repetitive, mundane responsibility, and the positives of ADHD sometimes come out later in life when you are able to pursue your passions.

When you were diagnosed with ADHD what were your thoughts?

I think I was in fifth year of medical school, very late. In fifth year, I wasn't doing very well, anxiety caught up with me, and one of the things people with [some people with] ADHD struggle with is they're more sensitive to anxiety, they have bad coping mechanisms. So, I started to look into why this was happening to me, and why I couldn't focus, why I couldn't bring myself to go in to lectures. It was weird that I wasn't able to do that when everyone else could.

Diagnosis for me was very important. It's important to remember that getting diagnosed doesn't necessarily mean you need medication. Sometimes a diagnosis on its own is enough to deal with your problems.

So, I started reading about it. With ADHD, you need to look at your childhood, it starts in childhood and tends to get better as you get older. And I realized I'd never paid attention at school, and that I'd possibly paid attention for about 10% of the time across the whole school year.

Nobody cared that I wasn't paying attention because I'd always do well at school. I'd go home two weeks before the exam and I'd cram everything. So, nobody cared, the teacher would look at me, I'd be making a paper airplane, but I was never disruptive because I had the inattentive type. A lot of boys get diagnosed with ADHD because they have the hyperactive type, and a lot of girls have the inattentive type and fall through the gaps. The inattentive type is the one who sits at the back of the classroom staring at the ceiling or falling asleep, and they tend to do badly because it never gets caught. So, if you're not disruptive in class and you're doing well the teacher doesn't care. I realized I was chronically bored.

I started off very hyperactive as a child, and then became inattentive. My mum would sit down and try to teach me at home what we were learning at school. She said that for an hour of trying to teach me I would spend fifty-five minutes on my feet, running from one end of the room, shouting out the answer and running back. I was seven or eight.

After that the only thing, my mum remembers of my childhood is that I was bored all the time. The way I dealt with it was by playing video games and by playing football.

Do you think it's a good idea for people with ADHD to play computer games?

Yeah absolutely. There's a lot of studies- I don't think there's a consensus- but there are lots of studies that show that actually computer games can make you smarter, depending on the genre. Because it's all just analysis, you're not using anything but your brain, and in a lot of the games you're trying to solve a puzzle in the game. It's not just sitting there, so it's good brain training.

Do you think that computer games can be over-stimulating, so that the threshold of what you find "exciting" is raised? And do you think that computer games replacing outdoors play may also be part of the problem?

That's a very interesting point, actually. There are a lot of theories about millennials being affected by the fact that we're used to instant gratification and surrounded by technology all of the time. The theories basically say that this instant gratification and constant stimulation has led to the formation of an ADHD-style personality in many people of the millennial generation, so it is entirely possible. It would be an interesting thing to research.

So, in the old days do you think that people with ADHD would have been outside making rabbit traps and climbing trees and doing something physically?

Yes, probably. The reason ADHD has now become a problem is because it doesn't fit with our schooling system. A hundred years ago people with ADHD would have been able to leave school at twelve and start working, do something with their hands or something artistic or entrepreneurial. But now you have to finish sixteen years of school. Which means that by the age of twelve you either get your attention span in order or it's you versus the school and there's something "wrong" with you, because you're not doing what 90% of the kids do.

So, do you like the idea of these new innovative schools like "woods schools" or "survival skills" schools where they teach kids outside and include crafts and survival skills, for example, to make lessons fun and exciting?

Yes, I like that very much, I've been researching that a lot actually. I know a lot of people have started home schooling their kids. I'm not saying it's necessarily a good thing. I don't know what the evidence is, but it's a different school model, which I find very interesting. If the learning is fun enough, some kids with ADHD are going to be able to get so excited about learning that they may be able to get obsessed with and hyper-focus on the teacher and learning, and then do very well.

What are your interests and achievements to date?

I found entrepreneurship before I knew I had ADHD. When I found out it made sense, because they call it the entrepreneurial disease.

I went to medical school and graduated as a doctor. Then I started an ecommerce business, which I stopped doing before it even launched. Then I jumped into the company which is still running today, which makes nutritional products, and that's doing very well. We sell our products across multiple countries through hundreds of outlets.

Tell me about your business ventures.

Funnily enough I started an ecommerce business which kicked off everyone in the family to go into business. I did achieve quite a lot as a 23 or 24-year-old, even though it never launched. We got our website ready, we got eight supermarkets onboard. So, the idea was we'd get supermarkets to use our portal to deliver groceries to people around them.

My family called me insane as I'd just finished medical school and never worked a day in my life, and I'd chase these CEOs for weeks. They'd ignore me and I'd find them eventually. I'd tell their secretaries that I was the CEO of our website business, and get the numbers of the CEOs, and eventually meet with them. I'd pitch them the idea with this awful PowerPoint presentation and they'd sign up. One of them kept calling me every week as they couldn't wait for the portal to launch.

My brothers saw this and got inspired and realized that if I was doing it they could do it too. So, we pooled our resources and skills and talked about what we could do, and realized there was a gap in the high protein diet market. We started to understand the psychology of the fitness dieter through Instagram and Facebook. It's a whole psychology.

Tell me about your technology ideas.

After I had success in my nutrition business, I wanted to go back into medicine; either as a doctor or healthcare technology related. My next idea, which is still in development, is basically a system which makes doctors more efficient on a daily basis, it's supposed to save you 20-30% of your time as a doctor. Which means you can see more patients and spend more time seeing priority patients.

[I] got accepted into [a doctor's entrepreneurship] scheme, where they took about 100 doctors out of the whole country. I had dinner at the Finnish ambassador's house, with all of these technology companies. It was the nicest food I've ever had- I've never had salmon so good in my life, I still dream of that salmon! But anyway, that dinner was a mixer for investors and entrepreneurs and medical technology companies to start ties. It was very interesting to be there and meet all of these important people.

So how would you say that you think?

I think I'm quite opportunistic, I don't know if it's my ADHD or not, but because I can learn something so quickly, that makes me a good opportunist. So, if I see a part of this industry that's lagging or just emerging and not mature as a market, then I can jump in, learn a lot about it and start doing it. I identify trends, see opportunities, and go for them. Which I think is a strength for a lot of people with ADHD, that's what they do. So, after I've gone online and read all about an industry, I can put it in a nice way that investors understand.

What challenges have you faced with your ADHD?

So, it's usually people around you, because you're almost on a different wavelength. The conversations go differently with people who are on the opposite side of the spectrum. People around you expect certain things from you that you have to do.

It hasn't affected me socially a lot as I hear or read it affects other people, but often children with ADHD are outcasts or they don't do very well in social situations.

I noticed children with ADHD- and I don't know if this is real or not or just a perception I have- but it seems to me like they're nicer. They have a lot of empathy, a lot of them. A lot of them can be a good sport about ADHD symptoms or other things that people do to them. But unfortunately, they don't always receive the same thing from everyone else.

As the result of maybe alienation or intense feelings kids with ADHD might respond by shutting down their feelings in order to manage them.

What kind of colleagues do you appreciate the most?

People who are flexible. A lot of highly educated people who know that one of the symptoms of ADHD is being disorganised will still tell you to get your shit together if you come in five minutes late. They won't have sympathy for you. It's one rule for everybody.

So, you do the positive things that ADHD enables you to do, that other people aren't doing, because of your hyper-focus or your ability to get more work done because you have excess energy- and they'll say, "oh thanks for doing that, that's amazing." But they don't want to take the positives and the negatives, they just want the positives. And its human nature to weigh the negatives things as more important that the positives, which is a cognitive bias.

Tell me about one thing at work you're proud of that you think ADHD traits have contributed to.

So, there was an alcoholic drug user who came in, who had been found on the floor and couldn't feel his legs. A lot of doctors would say that he's just drunk or high and they miss other symptoms. I did a neurological exam and it appeared that he was paralysed from the chest down.

A lot of patients who come in in this way are very unreliable historians, so you take everything they say with a pinch of salt, as it's often distorted. So, nobody believed him, my boss said that he was malingering and wanted a bed for the night (it was 4am), and that he was faking symptoms. But it didn't make sense that he was faking symptoms, because I did a full neurological examination of him and he'd have to have been a professional actor to have pulled that off.

By definition, to fake a lack of reflexes when I tested them, you need to tense your muscles. But this guy is floppy. Which means he genuinely had no reflexes. So, this told me he couldn't be faking. To my boss I was just a junior doctor trying to convince him of something that he was sure wasn't taking place.

But people with ADHD are often very prepared to argue their case against authority, rather than going along with something that they think is wrong. They also tend to be able to connect disparate pieces of information and make connections that people at the other end of the spectrum might not make. Spot patterns, make predictions, that kind of thing.

So, I said this to everyone. The nurse who had triaged the patient in, she was the first one to see him in the hospital and she thought he was faking as well, and she had twenty years of experience in A&E. My boss had ten years of experience. Maybe it made them a bit cynical.

Because this was an idea that I had invented, and nobody had thought about it, when I argued this, they followed protocol and said there was no evidence.

The charge nurse said that I only admitted him because I was too nice. But that wasn't it. I argued with my boss until he admitted him to have an MRI. We found out his spine was completely messed up. We didn't know if it was an autoimmune disease or something to do with his chronic drinking. But six hours after admission he went into respiratory arrest because his lung muscles stopped working, as the paralysis kept proceeding up and up until he couldn't breathe.

So, because I'm argumentative and because I came up with an unpopular theory on the spot, we managed to save his life. I don't know if that's related to my ADHD directly, but I know those two traits are quite common to a lot of people with ADHD: connecting the dots quickly, and arguing your case.

Describe your experiences at school.

I was very lucky that I learn quickly. But, if you've got ADHD and you've got higher IQ it can be worse because you don't get diagnosed. There's actually a correlation between your IQ and how late you are diagnosed. I struggled a lot, it was a difficult path. I almost failed med school a few times. At school, I didn't form long lasting friendships. Relationships are a big issue as well. ADHD affects every aspect of your life.

What about the label of ADHD affecting your outcome?

It depends on your personality. For me I think the label can make things worse because of other people knowing it. I think the label for me is very good for me to know. The point I want to make is in my opinion if two people with ADHD are equally talented, and one is diagnosed earlier, that person will have the better outcome.

Some people might find that the label has a negative effect on their confidence. But it depends on how you spin ADHD. If you describe it as a learning difficulty it can have a negative effect on your self-image. But even some psychologists and psychiatrists with ADHD prefer it to be argued that way, because it's a political thing. If you're in school and struggling and you need help, you're more likely for the government and activist groups to help you if you have a learning disability, not a super power. You're going to get more funding, more support at home because you have a learning disability. Do you understand what I mean?

I do, but I'm thinking of it the other way. There are studies that show that if people have more self-belief, they perform better, against people who are equally talented. If a teacher believes a student to be more intelligent than their peers, their attitude towards them boosts the student's performance. And so, labelling someone with a learning difficulty might really knock somebody's confidence and make them think that there is something wrong with them, when they're just good at different things.

So, the best possible outcome for this would be to diagnose someone, but explain that ADHD means that there are some things you will struggle to perform like other people, but then you'll have other positive aspects that other people don't have. The problem is that with the schooling system and many work places the way they are, you might get a lot of exposure to the things you're going to struggle with, rather than the things you're going to excel at. And this can give you the wrong idea about yourself. So, embrace the positive stuff, and try and find coping mechanisms for the negative stuff early on, before it starts affecting you.

Obviously as a doctor I've studied psychology and psychiatry so when I look at the outcome of a questionnaire I understand that there are positives and negative aspects. But a child or a layperson won't know that. So, when you sit down with a child it's important to explain this, because they won't know.

The hunter-gatherer theory has been widely disproved now, but it's still a good metaphor. There was a theory that ADHD traits were advantageous in hunter-gatherer settings, where hyper focus and a lack of fear during exciting or dangerous tasks would have been a very good thing. So, you can explain to them that thousands of years ago someone like them had the genetics of a hunter, so you would go out, hunt for the whole village and be the champion. And you'd go to war for your village, and perform very well strategically, you'd be a general at war, you'd defend your village. And obviously you're not going to be able to go out and fight a war or hunt and come back and have a great time doing laundry or, I don't know, patching up the roof of your hut. You're not going to have both personality traits.

So, explain they were made for different things?

Yeah. Everyone is made for different things.

ADHD is a disorder in terms of the context of society today. So, in psychiatry a lot of these disorders- depression, anxiety- one of the criteria for diagnosis is whether something is affecting your daily life. So, if ADHD is affecting your daily life, it's going to be called a disorder. And the problem is, everyone goes to school, most people have a job. So, if you're going to a normal school, or you're part of a normal school system, or you have a regular job that's not exciting enough, ADHD is going to affect your daily life.

If you could ask your teachers to change one thing what would it be?

I think the whole system needs to be changed because teachers are following rules. If you have a class of thirty and three or four kids have ADHD the teacher isn't going to be able to split the class into groups. There are a lot of different teaching systems. The approach of today is a teacher-centred approach, where students receive direct instructions from their teacher.

Another approach is student-centred approach, which is enquiry-based learning, which is good for children with ADHD, as they get to learn about things that interest them. The students decide what they want to learn about. They used to do that in America in forties, and then the war happened and they realised that Japan was better at technology that America, so one of their lobbying groups blamed it on the way they taught their students. So, they let go of the enquiry-based teaching, and they turned all of the schools into direct instruction teaching.

From then, everyone with ADHD suffered. The majority of kids were able to do well, because you're forcing kids to learn science and maths and languages, and everything that's good for society. But there's a group who get so disengaged that they drop out or look for thrills elsewhere, get addicted to drugs etc. A lot of these kids have ADHD. A saw a study the other day that looked at the prison population, and more than half met the criteria for ADHD.

So, it can be quite a dangerous thing to become bored in school if you have ADHD?

Yeah, because once something bad happens in your life, it's very easy to spiral. But people don't make the connection. But because you're impulsive, you may well end up doing something stupid eventually, if you don't have a passion to direct you towards something productive or positive.

What was your relationship like with your parents?

It was fine, growing up. My mum I have to give a lot of credit to my mum. If you have a child with ADHD it's very easy to give up. I did everything wrong. Everything in the parent's rulebook I did wrong. I never paid attention at school, I never tried to do my homework, I never stayed at home, I wouldn't sit on the couch for a second, I was just jumping around all over the place. All I wanted to do was play PlayStation, so my mum had to stop me from doing that. I wouldn't go to bed; my average bedtime would be about two am even as a ten-year-old. I made my parents feel like they were shit parents basically.

To normal parents who knew basic things about parenting the only things you have to do as a parent is make sure your child goes to bed early, eat their food- which also I didn't do all the time- and not spend hours in front of the TV. I wouldn't let my parents do any of them. But my mum persevered so much, I have to give her a lot of credit. She was extremely resilient. She took three weeks off work to teach me English so that I could retake an entrance exam that I had failed, to get into a British school. I was traumatised the first time I took it, I'd never felt so stupid in all my life, I didn't know any English, I didn't know what was going on. I remember crying at one point. But three weeks later I took it again and passed.

She used different mechanisms, like paying me to read. She manipulated me into doing it, by cutting down my pocket money and gave it back to me through reading, so I got hustled in a way. We used to get extra money every quarter based on our grades.

Do you think that encouraged your entrepreneurialism?

Maybe actually, yeah. Because you saw the reward. It's entirely possible.

Was there anything that your parents did that inspired you?

When you're a kid and parents do things that inspire you, you don't see it. But then you grow up and you realise in retrospect that were inspiring, like my mum.

My mum was a computer science teacher for a long time, and then she quit and started her own business. It was perfect. She had to be a mum and make money at the same time. So, she managed to start a business where she only had to work four months a year. And it made enough money for her to be completely independent, and put us through extra-curricular activities that cost a lot of money through the business. She still does that now. Works three or four months a year only.

Did that inspire you in terms of entrepreneurialism?

Yeah. I'm sure it gave me some sort of confidence. Because nobody walks out of medical school and jumps into starting a business. If I hadn't seen my mum do something similar growing up then I probably would have been more hesitant to do that.

So, it's like a seed that grows? Same as traveling, if you see your parents traveling around, it makes you want to do it.

Yeah anything. Music, business. And a lot of people around me started looking into business when I went into it. Because they realised that it's doable. If this person can do it, and we know him, then I can do it too.

That's what I thought when you started your nutrition business. I felt inspired, like I could do it too.

That's amazing. It's like a whole chain of people started doing it. And because small businesses are the backbone of the economy, you could almost have a campaign to improve the economy and better people's lives.

They should send entrepreneurs out to schools to do talks. Like young entrepreneurs who've made it at eighteen. To show all these kids, especially kids with ADHD, that okay, you're struggling now with your homework and your grades, but look, maybe you could do what I'm doing now.

Any other challenges at home?

Relationships were a big thing for me and can be for ADHD in general, so relationships with brother, parents. A lot of kids have Oppositional Defiant Disorder- it's the largest comorbidity of ADHD. I have that mildly. My brother had it a lot worse. In essence, you do the opposite of what your parents tell you, for no reason.

Challenges faced

Look at the statistics so you can avoid being a statistic. People with ADHD in jobs tend to move from one job to the next very quickly, get paid less. There's a lot of drug use, so be careful with that. I know a lot of people are against medicating their kids, but if they do medicate their kids there's a lower chance of them getting involved in drugs, and drugs will ruin your life. So, I'd say I'm pro-medication.

Other challenges in life are relationships, anxiety, stress. You have to manage your stress very well. Because you don't realise your stress creeps up on you. Some people don't make the connection between a stressful job and extra drinking on the weekend. But really, they're self-medicating. And they have no insight.

Insight is a very important word with ADHD and stress. Most people when they reach critical levels of anxiety and stress with no insight into how that's affecting their actions, and that's why they spiral out of control.

Actually, one of the criteria for discharging a mentally ill patient who has been sectioned and put into an inpatient mental health unit against their will, one of the criteria is making sure they have insight into their condition.

Because you know they're more capable of looking after themselves?

Yeah, exactly. The same thing happens on a microscopic level in everyday life with people who suffer from minor illnesses, like a bit of anxiety here and there, suppressed depression. It's very important to have insight into what your condition does to you, how to control it. The subclinical effects it has on your weekend or risk-taking behaviour. It's all connected.

Any other tips for people?

Yes. Obviously, I'm biased because I'm a doctor, but I would say when you're researching always stick to the facts. It's good to learn about things from different sources, but it's very important to look at what the recent research says. It's good to keep an evidence-based approach.

Kat Wczesniak

Founder of Curious Kat's Adventure Club (tour operator) and Xpertsm (social media marketing)

Age: 38   Industry: Travel and Social Media Marketing

ADHD Type: Combined

Walking into a room where Kat's around is like walking into a sunny conservatory. She's bouncy, uplifting, and disarmingly kind. The only person I've met who has built a viable business model around their bucket list, she wanted out of the conventional 9 to 5 lifestyle. She launched Kat's Adventure Club, to pursue her passion for travel, and five years later she reflects with me on what she's achieved.

Having come runner-up for the 2015 Best New Business award in the Federation of Small Businesses, you might forgive her if she assumed an air of arrogance or pomposity. But she's as down to earth and sweet as she's ever been, always speaking kindly and highly of others. But don't be fooled into underestimating her because of her well-meaning exterior. Underneath the smile, behind the obvious kindness, lurks a shrewd and driven woman.

Nowadays, you won't find her swooping round the dancefloor with an expression of glee on her face, you'll find her knuckling down at her desk, or letting off steam at her local Capoeira class. She's busy pouring herself into success with her second business, XpertSM, taking on the world of social media marketing, and has already been invited to speak at the British Library on the subject, within a year of starting the business.

I get the lowdown on the phenomenon of Kat Wczesniak, otherwise known as the very *Curious Kat*…

What are your thoughts about having ADHD?

I never considered I had it because I thought it was just about kids who run around and can't focus on anything. And while I am a bit hyperactive, if something interests me I can focus on it for hours, and spend a lot of time looking at things in depth. My current role requires spending long hours working on projects. However, you made me realise that one of the characteristics of ADHD is hyper-focus. That makes sense to me, as I often get completely sucked into a subject, and even get obsessed with ideas. I guess I was a bit shocked to discover that I have ADHD traits after doing the test, but after reading up about it, it really resonates with me. I hate boring jobs and tasks. I really can't stand them! I always find a way to put them off. But at the same time, there are things that I am extremely passionate about and can focus on for a long, long time without a break, or getting distracted. So, I found it interesting that ADHD can be thought of as difficulty shifting or controlling attention rather than a lack of attention.

I never thought I had any kind of disorder, if anything, it's the opposite, I've got an ability to do more than other people. Even yesterday as I was catching up with a friend, and told her about my last few weeks, she said: "Oh my god Kat, you've always been like a superwoman I don't know when you find time to do it all". I guess I just manage to pack a lot of activities into my day and do a lot of things. Once I set my mind to something, I will pull all the stops to achieve it, and I'm unstoppable. However, one thing is true, if I'm working on something boring, I make the silliest errors and cannot keep my attention on it for longer than few minutes. My mind just wanders.

What are your achievements to date, professionally?

I've built my tour operator business from scratch, with no investment, to a six-figure size. It was exciting enough to attract investment, which is now in process. I have had amazing, although exhausting few years jet-setting all over the world.

Last year, I started another company, working with digital marketing that is doing really well now too.

Looking back, if I thought it through in detail, I probably would not have decided to take up such risky and complicated line of work. However, being blessed with ADHD means that you just jump into tasks, rather than overthink them and the energy that comes from the passion for what you do lets you achieve the impossible. At the time, I just wanted to travel, meet people and experience new things, so I just did it!

I suppose one day I realised that I was stuck in an office, in a HR job I didn't love , complaining that I didn't have enough money or time to do what I was passionate about. .

To be fair you're either in a job where you're not paid enough to travel, or if you are paid enough, you don't have any time left. You know, one of those jobs where you pretty much work 60 hours per week.

I hate people who complain about things and do nothing to change them, and at that point I realised that it just didn't make any sense to continue this way. So, I started to think about how I can get around it, and what I could do to follow my dreams.

With Curious Kat's Adventure Club, I thought- this is what I want to do (trips, holidays, excursions), this is how I can cover my costs, by arranging paid trips, and it kind of just happened. I didn't even realise we were a tour operator until a few years in, you know

So, you realised you had a passion for travel, you followed your passion, and you built your life around it?

Yeah, pretty much. This is what happened. I've tried loads of different things. I studied psychology, and I worked in HR in organisations and even tried working in a clinical setting. And I initially thought I would enjoy the clinical psychologist career because I love people, but when I realised what it's like working in a hospital with people with mental issues, I realised it's not for me. I just don't have the patience. I'm very results oriented, very practical. If there is a problem, I think "let's find a solution." Let's not talk about it for hours and explore all the possible reasons, let's just focus on moving on and sorting it out. Well, needless to say I realised I wouldn't be a good psychologist. HR was a bit better, but it very constrained by law. And while the last company I was at was really amazing (we became one of the Sunday Times 100 Best Companies to Work For), I had some bad experiences of cut-throat environment where the HR's role was to hire and fire people, with no consideration for their wellbeing. I did not feel well being put in this position.

Travel was just it for me. I felt like fish in the water even though when I first started I had no experience of tourism, no education in this field or experience of running my own business. Someone said starting your own business is like jumping off a cliff and learning how to use the parachute on the way down. And that's pretty much what it was. You figure it out, you see problems, you resolve them. You learn.

In the first year, I had no idea what the business model actually was. I was just running trips, building the company up, traveling, meeting people and enjoying myself. Then at one point the director from the last company I worked at, offered to be my mentor. That was the turning point for me. I really admire what he achieved and it was great to be guided by him. He got me to read a few books and sign up for a few courses. He made me realise that, at that stage, I was doing almost everything by myself. So, I did not have a business, I had a job and not a very good one. So, slowly I made myself redundant from my business and brought other people in to run it. This allowed me to get the investment and to start my new business. Second time round it was much easier - within few months I had all the structures and processes in place, video tutorials, people.

So, was your business model for Curious Kat's Adventure Club based around your bucket list?

Yes, and following my passion really paid off. In 2015, I was a runner up for the Best New Business award in the Federation of Small Business awards. I also got a third place in the 'Entrepreneur of the Year' category.

Tell me about the challenges you've faced.

I think as your business grows the challenges grow as well. When I started I used to be quite worried about a lot of little things. However, as the time passes and you solve increasingly more complicated problems, you learn that you are able to come up with solutions, or more importantly that there is always a solution. It is a complete change in mind-set. You become comfortable with problems. Of course, there are things that still worry me, but they're bigger picture issues rather than little mishaps.

Can you describe your experiences of school for me?

I was one of those kids who was coasting most of the year and then catching up at the end of the year and pulling my grades up, when the exam time came. I was never able to just go at the same pace, be consistent and do all of the boring things. But I learnt quickly, so luckily, I had teachers who could see it and would show a degree of flexibility in allowing me to do catch-up tests at the end of the year.

It was also always easier to learn the subjects that I was interested in. When I see something as useless, I find it very difficult to study it. For example, I hated history because of the way they teach it in Poland. It was not about understanding the causality of events or wider politics (which would have been fascinating) - instead, they made us memorise dates, numbers of troops, names of battles. It was the most pointless exercise you can imagine. I always struggled in history exams.

If you could ask your teachers to change their teaching style what would it be?

I was reading about one of those schools, I think it's in Norway or Sweden where kids are learning things like physics and geometry through real life projects. So, they do not pick up subjects like maths or biology, they pick up projects, such as for example building a bicycle. And they're not just learning about the bicycle, they're learning about the mechanics, the physics, how the wheel works, and what pi is. Those schools put everything in context, so that it makes sense instead of teaching fragmented theories that have no practical implications.. For me, knowledge only counts if you can use it. Perhaps this is why in London I could learn languages effortlessly, just by hanging out and speaking with people, but at school declensions felt like quite a chore. Reciting the rules of grammar and actually understanding how the grammatical rules change the meaning are two different things.

At home, what was your relationship like with your parents?

My mum helped me with my schoolwork by making things more interesting. So, she would create little games based on my homework, which were brilliant. This is what helped me to really love some subjects. But I still hated the subjects she couldn't make interesting.

Do you have any examples?

I'm sorry darling, that was thirty years ago I don't remember in more detail!

Was there anything in particular that your mum did that inspired you?

I don't really know. She achieved a lot in her working life, but the times were quite different then. She worked her way up to a position of a director of the office of statistics in our region. But she had the idea that it's best to have a career and make steady progress. And I've realised at some point that when you have a job, you have an earning cap depending on the profession you choose, your boss, the sector you work in. But when you run your own business sky is the limit. Ok there is higher risk, and at times it is harder, but when you make it work there is no stopping you. As long as you keep learning and keep trying new things, of course.

So, I can't understand why people would want a job over running their own business. Most of them would be worried about the risk, however even when you're in a steady job, there are a lot of factors outside of your control. Your manager might change, with the new person in charge making the environment unbearable, or the company might go under. Either way, there is no stability. It's better to be in charge of your own destiny. Even if for a few years it might be difficult, eventually you are going to get there.

But, coming back to my mum, the times were different then, and in communist Poland there was no option of starting your own business. And in fact, my mum has achieved a position of high influence - public administrators had a lot of power in that system, they controlled a lot of resources and everyone wanted to be in their favour.

Apparently, a common comorbidity of ADHD is oppositional defiant disorder, where people directly defy authority as an automatic position.

Oh my god, I definitely have it then! I don't even like my GPS telling me what to do, I turn off the voice and just follow the map on the screen.. Otherwise it just gets on my nerves.

How would you advise your parents to deal with you to make it easier?

The thing is I didn't have any really big issues. It worked, it just worked in my own way. So instead of studying during the whole year I was just studying for the exams. My teachers were flexible enough to allow me to do catch-up tests. The school system is inherently wrong, but then that's a big curriculum change that would need to happen. And even if those in charge know it, it seems to be impossible to change it all at once. So, I guess a bit of flexibility and help in making the subjects interesting is the key here, until someone figures out how to tackle the big picture.

Alex H.
Affiliate advertiser, oil investor, gold and silver trader, imports

Industry: Gambling, commodities, crypto currency, imports

Age: 35

ADHD: Combined type

Be careful when you walk into a room with mister Humphreys. He's liable to rugby tackle you, empty out the contents of your hand bag, or throw you over his shoulder. You have to watch him like a hawk, and promptly instigate counter-moves. For twenty years, this big friendly giant has been randomly popping into my life and bringing with him a whirlwind of fun.

Alex probably leads the most nail-biting lifestyle of all the interviewees, making a living through high-risk investments and affiliate marketing. Despite this, he's incredibly down to earth and self-deprecating, insisting what he does is nothing special, rather than bragging or showing off about it. He genuinely has no idea that his ability to live well on his own accord is aspirational, albeit unpredictable and at times precarious.

He prefers an exciting way of life in sunny Tenerife off the coast of Africa, to the drab grey skies of London where our circle of friends grew up. Living in an apartment with a pool, surrounded by mountains and with a view of the sea. He enjoys the nightlife of the island and can socialize whenever he wants.

Always on the lookout for new ideas that will bring in the best return for his efforts, he's the ultimate high-risk opportunist. These days his portfolio of activities includes affiliate advertising for gambling, investing in oil, trading on the gold-silver ratio, stocks and shares and cryptocurrency.

Sociable, generous and fun, he's an exciting character to be around. Next move: maybe Malta, maybe not. Whatever it is, it'll be fun, he can assure you.

What's your experience of ADHD?

If I find a reason to be focused, I get really into things. If you don't find something that interests you, you're ***** really, aren't you!? I get really bored.

Tell me about what it was like for you, finding the things that you were interested in?

I don't know, you just fall into things. I was trading my shares. Mainly I was in oil. That market crashed while I was over living in Tenerife. I met a guy who does casino advertising and started working with him, building websites, advertising casinos. And we can make a lot of money. If someone registers through your site you make between 30 and 50% of their losses. The guy I work with once made £100,000 over two weekends. But it's a lot more difficult now. It's getting harder.

Before Casinos you were trading in oil?

Yeah, stocks and shares in oil companies.

What are you passionate about?

Where I think I can make some money really, is what I'm passionate about. They're all high risk, but good returns if it works out.

Do you find high-risk exciting?

When it goes well, yeah. But when it's going well, it's almost painful because it goes up and goes down. Yeah its' very exciting.

Is that quite addictive?

Mmm, yeah. When I was trading gold and silver, that's like leveraged, so that's borrowing money. Pretty much gambling. I was awake for four days once, because it's open 24 hours a day. I was addicted. When it went down it was too much. But you learn from that experience and decide not to do that *** any more.

So, I got into stocks and shares. Now I'm into casino advertising. It's much more reliable, and brings in a pretty high income.

Of all my interviewees, you seem to be the most hooked on adrenalin and high-risk.

I can't stand doing a regular job. I was temping and answering the phone and finding bits of paper. One day someone said to me "Are you feeling okay? You're not looking well" and I looked in the mirror, and my hair was all over the place, I looked absolutely dead. Haha. And I thought "I can't do this anymore!"

Was there someone in your family that was entrepreneurial that gave you an example to follow?

Yeah, my dad was into investments and imports. So that really got me into it, that's what gave me the idea.

Do you tend to just jump in?

Yeah, but if you're investing, just start off small. Also, you have to think differently, if you do the same as everyone else you're not going to make any money.

Tell me about your school experience.

I got in loads of trouble at school. I don't know why. No, I do know why. Hahaha! I was doing quite well when I got kicked out. I went to a school for dyslexics. I think that helped me. But I got suspended for smoking and then I got expelled.

Then I dropped out of uni. I didn't like the subject and after a year I thought that I couldn't do another two years. So, I went to work for my dad in London.

It's funny because your tastes change over time. If you get something that makes you take an interest in something, like a good teacher, then you like a subject, but if not, it can make you really hate it. I didn't really like history at school, but now I like it a lot.

It's about finding what interests you. If you don't know you like the subject and you have people telling you to like it, it's not going to work. You don't do your homework and you get in trouble.

So, what was your relationship like with your parents?

Well with my mum, she was worried about me too much, they can get concerned about you and your direction in life. But you need to do what you want to do. .

What's next for you?

I'd say I'm only just finding my path now, but before I never really knew what I was going to do. But now, four things have fallen into place, and it's good because it's a lot more secure.

I'm also investing in Crypto currency. Basically, there's one called Neo Coin, backed by Microsoft and Ali Baba. We just put in an investment last night. Now that I've got four income streams; the casinos, crypto currencies and shares, it allows me to spread my risk. You should always be bringing in some decent revenue if you have enough income channels.

Ray Weer
Property Developer   Industry: Real Estate

Age: 37   ADHD: Combined Type

Ray is an engaging character. I don't know him well, having met him as a potential investor in one of his properties, but he took me on a tour of his city and showed me another five renovation projects he had going, without pausing for breath once. With exacting standards and ingenious solutions for durability, his properties stand out, neck and shoulders above the competition.

I asked him if he had ADHD, and if he would like to be in my book, and he looked shocked, and asked me "how did you know?" As with other ADHD'ers, he got into trouble at school, before finding his passion in adulthood, becoming obsessed with property and subsequently finding success.

Ray mainly dreamed of traveling and earning money through rental property when he left education, that would allow her to travel indefinitely. But instead he became hooked on "flipping houses" rather than renting them out, and going on numerous holidays every year.

When were you diagnosed with ADHD, and what were your thoughts on the diagnosis?

I was diagnosed back in primary school, and I was really shocked. I was doing pretty well in school but I was always getting in trouble for being disruptive and lairy. I'd heard about it before but I thought it was a load of b****, that it couldn't possibly be me, because I get a lot done when I want to.

I really love what I do. I wake up in the morning and the first thing I do is check my phone, check Right Move [a property purchasing website] for alerts and new properties on the market.

What are your achievements to date?

I own about fifteen properties that I use for rental income, and then I develop and sell on others. At the moment, I just bought an old people's home that I'm developing into one and two-bedroom units. I go on about 10 holidays a year. A lot of people that I know want to get into property because they can see that you organize your own time and you get to be your own boss. Who doesn't want that?

When I saved up for my first house everything went to plan, in terms of timing and I was pleased about that, because I tried really hard to reach my target on time. The only thing I wanted to do was go traveling, get out there and enjoy life, and then invest in property and get rental income, to sustain a life of traveling. I used to fantasize about just jumping in my car and driving away.

Describe your experience of school

I didn't really like school, I wasn't stupid I could just never sit still, hated half the subjects, they seemed so pointless. I got suspended. At one point, I had to change schools. But I did well. I never did my homework or studied until it came to the end of the year at exam time, but I always came more or less at the top of the class in any subject that I was interested in. I was very annoying like that. Always in trouble but I got good marks. I think the teachers hated me. Haha.

I think it was because my mum taught us from a very young age to be competitive at learning. I don't know how. But she used to spend a lot of time with us when we were little so that we really enjoyed it when we got something right. We got a lot of praise. So, getting something right was really fun. I was that really annoying kid who had my hand up at every question in the subjects that I liked, but I would get frustrated when they wouldn't pick me. I still couldn't make myself do my homework. Homework was a nightmare.

What was your relationship like with your parents?

I was kind of a naughty kid. I loved my parents but I guess I was a bit of a handful. I never stole or anything, but I never really did what I was told. I think they had their work cut out with me.

My dad was really nice. He used to laugh a lot and make everybody laugh. When we got a bit older I had a few problems with my mum. You couldn't win. And for me, if I can't win and there's no way to at least be heard or get my point of view across, fairly… if that's not going to happen for me, then I won't take part. So, I stayed out of the house and got into trouble with my mates.

Because if the dice are loaded against me, and I will not take part in any form of conversation, debate or competition where the dice are loaded against me. In a parent-child relationship, obviously the dice are loaded against you. They're the boss. But, they're not always right. For me, it's always been the merit of the argument that should win, not a title that is just given, which is what a parent is. If you can't win the debate logically having listened to what I have to say, then I shouldn't have to do what you say. Also, I didn't want to be told what to do.

My mum would always ask me to tidy up. And I'd think, why? My main problem with people who are obsessed with tidying up is that there is no reason anymore. They might like it tidy (which is subjective) but the fact that it bothers them is illogical. So long as you're not spending more time looking for something than you're spending tidying, you're more time-rich. We evolved to tidy things up to organize our world so that we could be productive, figure things out, get rid of disease, and all these things. None of this is relevant anymore. And if we don't need things to be tidy in order to be productive, then the instinct is no longer helpful, its unhelpful. Nowadays, the shoes are on the other foot. If one of my tenants leaves the place in a mess when they leave, I absolutely screw.

My other problem with my mum making so much of an issue out of it, is because it felt to me that she would rather have a clean house than chill out and have a good relationship with me. It felt like she valued something that is utterly pointless more than something really important. I used to wish she's been a bit more easy-going. But then I guessed she wishes that I'd been a better son! Maybe she wins!

See, people don't understand that. For people with ADHD their cost-benefit analysis of tidying is different. Someone with ADHD is going to have to make a lot more effort to keep things tidy. Not only do they not put things away as they go so they'll have to tidy up more often, tidying up is also more painful. So, the cost-benefit analysis is not worth it to be tidy. Especially when for someone with ADHD the benefit of having a tidy house is often not that high, because they're in their head rather than in the moment.

Well it's funny you say that, because now as an adult, I like tidying. I enjoy it because I can think about other things.

But when I was a kid, I didn't care. And there was someone there making my life hell about it.

Yeah, it's true. But I guess some people have a little touch of OCD as well. And just like we can't stand to tidy, they can't sit in an untidy room. My mum has the same thing.

Yes, that's very true. But at least the ADHD approach comes from an efficiency approach. You get more time to spend on important things. Dishwashers provide the perfect example of how most of the world sees things differently from people with ADHD. I used to use my dishwasher as a cupboard, which was the easiest thing in the world, and it made absolutely no difference except a good one.

That's what I do! But people who live with you won't appreciate that. It's the norm. You can't tell people, that's how the world works.

But why are they wasting their time putting things in the cupboard? It doesn't make any sense.

You can't just fight against the norm with everyone.

I will if they're wrong.

It's going to make your life a lot more difficult.

Thankfully my wife has a lot of ADHD traits as well, so when I realised that I thought "Thank god! She's not going to get angry with me."

Oh, that's great. That's the thing, people with ADHD celebrate this stuff, like when you find out that someone is messy. No one else would understand that.

It works great for me, because I know I still have to keep it pretty tidy out of respect, but I know she's not going to throw a hissy fit if I forget something.

Was there anything in particular that your parents did that inspired you?

I remember seeing my dad lose his job and getting depressed and thinking that I never wanted that to happen to me. Things were pretty difficult in terms of money for a while. Then he got a job working for a man who renovated houses. That was what got me into the idea of it. A few years ago, my dad had a little bit of savings and we realized that if he'd invested it in houses he could have made a fortune. So, he gave it to me to invest, and after he got his money back in a few months, he realized it was easy money, and he gave me it back to make him some more. Same with my aunt and some other people in my family, some friends.

What really excites you?

Call me obsessed but I'm mad for what I do. After I did my first property, and I made about 30k in a few weeks by buying a house, renovating it and flipping it for profit, and I saw that money in my bank account I was hooked. And I love it. I'm really a stickler for the details too, I have a really high standard, everything has to be perfect. Now I'm going bigger and better.

What's next?

What, after this one? Even bigger!

Veronica Roan

Founder of Roan web design agency, investor, auctioneer

Industry: Education, sales, content

Age: 36

ADHD Type: Moderate Inattentive Type

I've known Veronica since we were teenagers, and she's endearingly eccentric, but doesn't really know why. When we went to dinner for this interview, all she wanted was a plate of plain chicken thighs. As it turned out she'd stopped by McDonalds on the way, and eaten four cheeseburgers. Perplexed about why I started laughing, her innocence and good intentions are endearing (if a bit frustrating) to say the least.

At least she's eating properly now. A year ago, she had lost so much weight during one of her healthy-eating crusades she looked worryingly under-nourished. She was so excited to share her discovery that the calorie content of food also matters, and not just the volume of food you consume. The gallons of blended spinach and lemon grass she'd been drinking hadn't been enough to sustain her, it would seem. I worry about her sometimes.

Veronica runs her own web design agency, and as such is all about crisp lines and sleek design, noticing them in everything and everywhere she goes. She can always tell you how an environment or building might be improved and made cleaner, and it's fascinating to see how her brain works. She also invests in property and commodities, and buys and sells at auctions. These achievements satisfy her somewhat, replacing her earlier ambitions to win a Nobel peace prize, come up with her own religion, invent a way to time travel and summarize existence in one word. This out of the box thinker is full of unusual ideas, and a refreshing perspective on life.

Tell me about your achievements to date.

I'm really proud of my web design agency which is my main focus at the moment. I have a few clients, some big and some small. I work really hard and I really enjoy it. I can work on a design all day and not even notice that its night time and I haven't eaten anything or drunk anything.

I kind of just fell into it after I started freelancing while I was travelling in China. One thing led to another and I couldn't take all the jobs that came in, so I had to hire freelancers to take some of them. That was how I started my agency, it wasn't planned it just kind of happened. Now I'm trying to let go a little bit more, so I've hired a manager so I can think about starting another business, and I'm researching my options, I'm not really sure what just yet.

Maybe stay away from a nutrition business, or you might end up starving your customers.

Yes, very funny. At least I was eating healthily. Do you want me to tell you about my achievements or not?

[Prolonged arguing has been edited out]

Anyway. Apart from the web design company, one of the biggest achievements in my mind is the traveling I did. I always believed you work to live rather than the other way around, and experiencing life is about getting out into the world and seeing it. After I finished university I had a few years in a design studio in a marketing agency. But it was really, I just couldn't do it, going in every day, sitting with people. I get quite anxious. I didn't have any creative freedom, I had to do everything to budget and to deadlines and it was really stressful and boring. I didn't really get on with the other people in the agency. Once they all went to the pub and didn't even tell me they were going.

One day I had to get up at 5am to go to a meeting in Brussels about this big website that then got cancelled. I don't know why, but that felt like the final straw to me, it felt like I wasn't in control of my life. So, rather than just sitting in the box that I thought was expected of me I left and went traveling, and I felt free. It's good to get out and see the world.

So, you didn't follow a straight-forward career path?

No, not really, it was a quite convoluted.

What kind of colleagues did you like, when you had a job?

Flexible ones. Where the arrival times and departure times are flexible, so long as you put in the hours and achieve the results expected of you. Which I always did, and more.

People who realize that an idea that changes the profitability of an entire business model, is more important than being a bit late for a meeting or forgetting to reply to an email on the same day. Some things affect profitability, and others don't.

How was your life at school?

I did have some friendship problems at school, everyone seemed so bitchy, and it kind of put me off women for a while. I guess they thought I was strange. I started truanting for a bit when I got older because I got really fed up of going in every day, but my parents started taking me to school, so I couldn't get out of it. Once I ran into my dad in the supermarket when I was meant to be in school. He was really angry, but it was just one day.

What about entrepreneurialism? Are you opportunistic?

I am, I like to research opportunities, but sometimes I hesitate too long before I do something, so that means I can miss out. I am quite risk-averse, but I'm learning to get over that.

When I was a kid I sold crisps at school for double the price that my mum had bought them for. My mum couldn't believe where all the crisps were going, and thought we were all really hungry, so she kept buying more. I over-complicated it though by trying to get my sister to help but she just told my mum. I should have paid her a bit better!

What are your passions?

Design. Technology. Having a simple, clean life. I think a lot about how I can be a better person.

What's next for you?

I'm not sure, I need to think about it. There are lots of different directions I could pursue. I want to make sure I choose the right one. I don't want to act prematurely.

"Liz"

Pioneering entrepreneur, founder of clinical research matching agency

Age: 57   Industry: Healthcare research

ADHD Type: Combined

Case study only, currently unavailable to interview

Liz is my ultimate hero, she's who I look up to and would love to be more like. When I met her to interview for a job, I developed a lady-crush that I've never really gotten past. My colleagues tried to be polite, but I'm sure they found it a little sickening. But I really couldn't help myself.

She pioneered the entire patient recruitment agency, starting the first agency of its kind to match up patients with research projects. She grew the company for thirty years from sole-trader status to a team of forty-six people, working for clients around the globe. Multi-million-dollar projects were typical, with assets amassing to millions of dollars.

Knowledgeable, funny and intensely charismatic, she finds a wealth of topics fascinating. She'll believe in you, trust you, be devastated that you didn't live up to her expectations, and then fight to bring you up to her exacting standards, giving you a world of opportunities as you go.

These days, semi-retired and planning her next move, she jet-sets around the world, visiting her equally international sons and granddaughter.

Unfortunately, Liz can be excruciating to get hold of, and I'm yet to interview her. I realised quite quickly whilst researching this book that conducting interviews with ADHD'ers might present an interesting logistical challenge! They're not always the most available or responsive people to say the least. For now, I'm including her synopsis, because her story is so compelling, and will include her interview when she decides to surface for air (whenever that may be).

Watch this space

Are there positive sides to ADHD?

In the professionals' sphere, there's a debate raging about whether to call ADHD a set of personality traits, a disorder, a learning disability or my preference, "pioneering-entrepreneur's disease." Okay, okay, I'm saying this with more than a hint of humour, but it certainly seems apt where my interviews are concerned.

There's an enormous rigmarole of politics, big-money pharma and educational debates involved. Which is hardly surprising considering the drugs market is predicted to reach $14 billion by 2024. That's a lot of money to argue over! Pills over here please!

Dry, sarcastic humour put to one side for a moment (I did work for big pharma once-upon-a-time and I'd hate to get sued), the interviews left me with a sense that some ADHD characteristics can potentially bring great advantages in life, if harnessed. When combined with enough self-confidence to take a chance on something that "sparks a fire" inside, it looks like a recipe for success for some people.

The Gift of Hyper-Focus

In terms of attention, all of the stars in this book described how they are able to focus for extended periods of time on novel, "interesting" or exciting activities, often getting a great deal done in a short period of time. Conversely, they seem unable to pay attention to boring or "mundane" things for long. They've all found success by using their natural areas of interest as a basis for how they make a living.

The advantages of hyper-focus, and avoiding excessive boredom, is an interesting area to be considered by the ADHD community. Perhaps exploring the idea that ADHD brains are attracted to different things might lead to a more advantageous approach than trying to make everyone be interested in all subjects.

Property developer Ray couldn't conceal his excitement for what he does every day, explaining that when he wakes up in the morning the first thing he does is grab his phone and check for property alerts for new opportunities. He became visibly animated when he told me how he became addicted to property renovation after he "made about 30k in a few weeks by buying a house, renovating it and flipping it for profit." "I saw that money in my bank account and I was hooked."

Interestingly, from the accounts I received, hyper-focus seems to change an ADHD'er into a "stickler for the details" in their area of expertise- which is the complete opposite from their inattentiveness in areas that don't interest them. "I'm really a stickler for the details too, everything has to be perfect." Ray told me.

Bubbly business-woman Kat described the relationship between inattention and hyper-focus perfectly during her interview, by telling me how much she can't stand to do things she finds boring, always finding a "way to put them off." Contrastingly, she finds she can focus for extended periods of time, without a break, on activities that she is really passionate about:

> "If something interests me I can really focus a lot, and I can really spend a lot of time looking at things in depth, spend a lot of hours working on a project. The thing that I found interesting about ADHD is that one of the subjects of it is hyper-focus. You get completely sucked into a subject, you are just thinking about that and getting obsessed with that."

It seems that in areas of hyper-focus, ADHD becomes an advantage for our superstars. Doctor Mo explained that for him, hyper-focus allowed him to be entrepreneurial and opportunistic, learning a lot about a subject quickly so that he can jump in and cater to emerging trends.

The key seems to be that the way in which they make a living, are founded in their areas of hyper-focus, which has greatly contributed to their success.

The Gift of Energy and Excitement

At the end of the interviews, it seemed to me that all of our ADHD'ers pour abundant energy into their passions. Kat described how she has so much energy behind her that she would never think she had any kind of disorder, quite the opposite. To her, her energy enables her to do "more" than other people. She recalled recently being called a "superwoman" for doing so much with her time by a friend. "I just find a lot of time to pack a lot of activities into my day and do a lot of things," she told me.

Of everyone, no one takes greater advantage of their gift of super-human energy than journalist, magazine founder and content agency founder, Kyle. Kyle is so proud of his ADHD, that he highly recommends it to others. Whilst he seemed to be "tongue-in-cheekily joking," I have no doubt that he was simultaneously completely serious.

As we've seen, he thinks ADHD is one of the reasons he's been able to achieve so much: "without that level of ADHD driving and underpinning the energy that I'm putting into this [his businesses], I'm not sure I'd have been able to achieve a lot of the things that I've done in my life."

From his perspective, ADHD can be a gift, because he's mastered it and channelled it, and found pursuits that deeply excite him. He uses mindfulness and positive thinking to always be aware of his options, and help him make the right decisions. From here, he feels he's been able to achieve a lot of things that his peers weren't able to, using his energy to go "above and beyond." Carrying this attitude across to his professional life has allowed him to work tirelessly day-in and day-out for months on end, without feeling run down or tired, just giving it his all and running with it:

> "It's about finding something that lights a bit of a fire within you, and then just going with it. The energy that you can create around that is endless."

According to Kyle "ADHD is about grabbing hold of an idea that you're excited about, and channelling all your energy into that. And it's amazing what you can achieve."

The Gift of Independent Thought

As we've seen from doctor Mo's interview, independent thought can be life-saving. Independent thought is arguably the driving force behind technological and social evolution. Inventors, political activists and entrepreneurs must think outside the box to be successful.

Our stars have used their gift of independent thought to question the status quo, with some astonishing results. Doctor Mo saved a homeless man's life by refusing to follow standard protocol and discharge him from hospital, Ray decided he needed to be in charge of his own destiny, Kyle adamantly educated himself making it entirely on his own, Alex broke free of expectations and makes a living through investments and Kat rejected employment and travelled the world instead.

Although it could be a coincidence that my friends tend to think for themselves, it suggests that it may be a common quality for people with ADHD. As adults, this appears to have been extremely beneficial, whereas for my interviewees as children, this quality sometimes got them in trouble with the school system or their parents.

Personally, I can't get enough of how doctor Mo saved a homeless man's life by questioning the 'normal' medical protocol. Not only this but he stuck to his guns against a wall of pressure, arguing his case against cynical authority figures with many years of experience.

When an alcoholic drug-user presented at the Accident and Emergency department as paralysed from the neck down, Mo's medical team believed him to be faking the symptoms, to get a bed for the night. Mo, however, thought for himself and had a different conclusion. After performing a full neurological examination, he theorized that the patient would have been unable to fake his symptoms.

> "By definition, to fake a lack of reflexes when I tested them, you need to tense your muscles. But this guy is floppy. Which means he genuinely had no reflexes. So, this told me he couldn't be faking. To my boss I was just a junior doctor trying to convince him of something that he was sure wasn't taking place."

Without Mo possessing a high degree of independent thought, combined with tenacity, the patient would surely have died when he suffered sudden respiratory arrest six hours later. Standing up to the entire medical team, with thirty years' experience combined, Mo argued his logical case.

> "This was an idea that I had invented, and nobody had thought about it, when I argued this, they followed protocol and said there was no evidence.
>
> I argued with my boss until he admitted him to have an MRI. We found out his spine was completely messed up. Six hours after admission he went into respiratory arrest because his lung muscles stopped working, as the paralysis kept proceeding up and up until he couldn't breathe."

Mo told me he wasn't sure if the incident is directly relatable to his ADHD, after all, where does a person stop and a 'symptom' begin? But he described how people with ADHD are often very prepared to argue their case against authority, rather than going along with something that they think is wrong. He also believes that ADHD'ers are often able to think creatively, connecting disparate pieces of information and making connections that people at the other end of the spectrum might not make, "spot patterns, make predictions, that kind of thing."

With an additional soul gracing our planet, I don't think there can be any greater case for independent thought as an advantage.

The Gift of Bravery

Impulsivity is one of the characteristics of ADHD. Looking closely, after a few life lessons have been learnt and a few cuts and scrapes earned, this could be reframed as bravery, for our superstars. Despite at times feeling anxious and fearful, it appears they will take the plunge to make decisions that are right for them.

Kat described how she realised she had a passion for travel, followed it, and built her life around it. She relished the first year of Curious Kat's Adventure Club, but started it having "no idea what the business model actually was. I was just running trips, building the company up, traveling, meeting people and enjoying myself."

> "I thought- this is what I want to do [trips, holidays, excursions], this is how I can cover my costs, by arranging paid trips, and it kind of just happened. I didn't really think about it, it just happened. I didn't even realise we were a tour operator until a few years in, you know."

When Kat started her adventure club she worried about lots of little things. She quickly learnt that she was able to come up with solutions, that there is "always a solution." Over time, and now on her second business, she has experienced "a complete change in mind-set. You become comfortable with problems. Of course, things still worry me, but they're bigger picture things rather than small things."

> "Someone said starting your own business is like jumping off a cliff and learning how to open the parachute on the way down. And that's pretty much what it was. You figure it out, you see problems, you resolve them. You learn."

Investor Alex capitalizes investigates investment opportunities and assesses if it's worth his time. "They're all high risk, but good returns if it works out," he explains. Despite sometimes feeling anxious because of the danger of his investments going down in value, he's learnt how to moderate his risks by spreading them across multiple platforms. In this way, he's able to continue making a living through investments, rather than conforming with a conventional lifestyle.

> "When I was trading gold and silver, that's leveraged, so that's borrowing money. Pretty much gambling. I was awake for four days once, because it's open 24 hours a day. I was addicted. When it went down it was too much. But you learn from that experience and decide not to do that *** anymore."

The Gift of Tenacity and Drive

When you combine hyper-focus, excitable energy, independent thought and bravery, the resulting tenacity looks like an unstoppable force in some of my friends. When freely applied during adulthood, the results can be impressive.

Kyle is no stranger to sticking to his guns tenaciously, throughout his life. His description of his time at school gave me the distinct impression that he was fighting for his very identity. That if they'd "broken" him he'd have lost a part of himself, and never quite been the same. In the battle of Kyle versus "pigeon hole," Kyle won, and he's still winning to this day. We'll delve into this battle later, in the schooling section.

Kyle's tenacity shines through in several of his stories. My favourite is of a young journalist working for "rowdy" titles, proposing "insane" article ideas, refusing to be tempered or tamed. "Most people who don't have ADHD, would have an insane idea, and would never do anything with them" he says. "I actually went and did them." Despite a sea of disbelief from his friends and colleagues, Kyle proudly recalls how "nothing would have stopped me" from going through with his ideas.[1]

Similarly, tenacious, I got the impression that doctor Mo was chomping at the bit to follow his entrepreneurial instincts when he finished his education. As soon as he graduated from medical school he jumped straight into starting his first business in ecommerce "which kicked off everyone in the family to go into business." Despite having no experience, doctor Mo chased down the CEOs of large-chain supermarkets and signed eight of them up to his digital platform, which provided a grocery delivery service. His tenacity came to the fore, despite disbelief- which later turned to awe- from his family:

> "My family called me insane as I'd just finished medical school and never worked a day in my life, and I'd chase these CEOs for weeks."

He recalled how he would be ignored, but how he kept going, persistently chasing them and signing them up eventually. Eventually doctor Mo became an inspiration to the rest of his family, and now he and his brothers sell high protein products across multiple countries from more than a hundred retail outlets.

As a child, Mo showed similar tenaciousness when it came to resisting structure, discipline, learning and control at home. Refusing to sit still, jumping around and "doing everything wrong." His mother showed great resilience when it came to imposing order, teaching him and incentivising him to learn.

The stories of Kyle and Mo make me question what it would be like to be a parent or teacher, and how to choose the best approach for an ADHD child. These are difficult questions to answer when a child needs to learn how to be safe, how to behave within society, and of course needs to be educated.

Immediately I take their side and see things from their point of view. But when I think about it, I'm pretty sure I would have sat and eaten chocolate all day if I had been able to get away with it. What a terrible care strategy, if I had been allowed. And yet if I was tenacious and driven to rebel as a child, how could the adults in my life have taught me what I needed to know, without breaking my will or boring me half to death?

It sounds like a difficult road to navigate so that ADHD'ers who may be tenacious, rebellious children can be free, creative and successful people, able to follow the path that they choose. We delve into these ideas in more detail in the schooling and parenting sections.

Can ADHD be harnessed?

Finding and Channelling Passions

As we heard from Kyle earlier, for him, the key to success with ADHD is about finding and channelling a passion that lights a fire in you. Could the consequences of not finding a productive passion, result in some people "falling through the gaps?"

What did my interviewees advise for ADHD'ers looking for their passions? Doctor Mo explains that not everyone with ADHD are going to enjoy doing the same things. "Not everyone with ADHD is going to love to code [computer programs], or love horse riding, or playing sports, but they are all going to get obsessed with something."

"ADHD is not necessarily the inability to focus, it can be the inability to shift your focus from one thing to something else. It's not a lack of attention, it's a lack of being able to control your attention. That's why people who tend to get their attention stuck on something productive tend to do very well."

Some people with ADHD seem to know from an early age exactly what they're passionate about. In Ray's case, the only thing he wanted to do was renovate and rent out property. Alex, on the other hand, described how for him he would just "fall into things" and that his interests "change over time." "I didn't really like history at school, but now I like it a lot. It's about finding what interests you." According to Alex, trying to force an interest in something can backfire, and create a lot of resistance. Kat, Kyle and Veronica similarly find that their passions evolve and change.

At school, Kyle loved music and English, but was unable to focus on these areas until he left school and became a musician. Despite loving music, he told me "it wasn't until I got into journalism that I had a professional goal to channel my energy into." And yet he still finds time to play in two different bands. He acknowledges that finding the subjects ADHD'ers are interested in can be difficult at a young age:

> "I appreciate that perhaps as a fourteen-year-old, you aren't going to find your passion points just yet, but, there will be things with any kid that they are passionate about.
>
> With ADHD kids, it comes back to finding and acknowledging a passion, anything with that, the options are endless. You can just go to the very, very, very top. Being able to distinguish this at a young age, it's difficult."

Doctor Mo suggests reading as a good way to cover a large range of subjects and then "decide if it's something that could spark an 'obsession,' and then try it in real life." But he warns that if the ADHD'er at hand doesn't enjoy reading, they may have to incentivized in some way, or simply try it in real life. "People with ADHD are good at covering a large spectrum of different subjects very quickly and picking up on what will interest them" he advises.

He describes how he's been chasing the "flow" state- a state of happiness that you enter when you are deeply engaged in something- for his entire life. "Flow" state, as described by Mihal Csikszentmihalyi, in his book "Flow: The Psychology of Optimal Experience," and demonstrated by the graph below, can be entered into when the level of challenge of a task at hand matches up well with the skillset of an individual to perform a task well, whilst still being mentally stimulated.

According to Mo, flow is "when you're enjoying what you're doing because you have the skillset not to struggle with an activity, and to do it well, but the activity is challenging enough to be engaging, without being so challenging that it's exhausting."

Practicing medicine is a perfect example of how a job can induce flow state, or miss the mark and leave you bored or stressed:

> "If you're a consultant doing the job of a junior doctor, you're over skilled and the job won't be challenging enough to engage you, you'll be below flow state. For a junior doctor to perform a consultant's role would be anxiety-provoking, and they wouldn't have the skillset so again- out of flow state. A good match is needed for any hobby or job to be stimulating. If you get your job and a hobby in which you have a flow state, you're fine in life. What else do you need?"

Passions of the Superstars

All of our superstars show strong entrepreneurial traits. They've rejected the standard workplace to some degree and are excited by following their own business ventures, including tour operators, content and marketing, journalism, investments, medical tech and property.

Other passions held by our superstars, which could be a good place to start looking for inspiration, are an interesting mix of high-brow, as well as hedonistic pursuits. These include travel, music, sport, science, philosophy, history, politics, Russian literature and psychology, to name but a few.

In my next book '100 Fun Ideas to Harness ADHD' I'll be exploring games and activities for finding and encouraging the natural passions of ADHD children, such as entrepreneurialism, art, sports, travel and creative problem solving. You can find two examples at the end of this book. If you'd like to be notified when it is released, email me at: rachel.knight.books@gmail.com

How did ADHD affect school?

Our superstars mostly had negative opinions of the school system as being oppressive, and disadvantageous to people with ADHD. Kat told me "the school system is inherently wrong," and she believes this is so obvious that everybody knows it. She's in no doubt that "a big change needs to happen at one point. We all know that, but it costs money as it's the whole big picture that needs to change."

According to doctor Mo "the whole system needs to be changed because teachers are following rules." He's convinced that in today's teacher-centred schooling approach- where students receive direct instructions from their teacher -ADHD is "usually going to have a negative impact," despite some people using the positive side of ADHD to help them in life.

Mo spent his entire school career chronically bored, and daydreamed of playing football and computer games to get him through each day:

> "In terms of school, the only way I got through school every day was by playing football. I'd go in, wait for four hours just thinking about lunchtime. At lunchtime, I wouldn't eat I'd go and play football. So that was the highlight of my day. Then when football was done I would sit through four or five hours of school so I could go home and play PlayStation. My whole world revolved around that."

Kyle is concerned that schools often aim at pumping out cookie-cutter people, failing children because they place more emphasis on following the rules than on encouraging their minds to blossom:

> "There's no infrastructure within the system to encourage individuality, it's not there to encourage creativity, it's almost pushing kids through this funnel, and if you're not careful as a child, you're going to come out the same as everybody f***ing else, right? And you're just going to be another f***ing workforce person to go out into the world and work nine to five and come home and watch television, and have dinner and then wake up and

then go to work, come home, watch television. And you're never going to live your life."

He recognises that it can be a hard balancing-act to ensure a wide-range of education whilst encouraging specialities in the education system, but that too often the focus is on trying to make all children, like all subjects. Instead of allowing children to focus more on their passions and gifts, they're treated the same as other children. He pointed out that his brain worked differently, but when he acted differently, he was punished.

For ADHD children, can the system dissuade their gifts by encouraging them to follow the status quo? Are they at risk of losing their individuality, and living their lives in accordance with expectation, rather than being true to who they are?

These insights beg the question of what would have been possible for my friends in schools that engaged them with their passions, and took a different approach to learning.

Alternative Schooling Systems

Some interviewees have been considering alternatives to the current schooling system. Kat has been reading about problem-based learning systems in Scandinavia, and is impressed by their approach:

> "I was reading about one of those schools, I think it's in Norway or Sweden where kids are learning things like physics and geometry and things using projects. So, they are doing things like learning to build a bicycle. And they're not just learning about the bicycle, they're learning about the mechanics, the physics, how the wheel works. Those schools put everything in context so it all makes sense instead of learning everything out of context as though it is useless information. Then it's just dry theory. For me, knowledge was always about things that are useful, when you get to use it."

Like Kat, Mo is also very interested in new and innovative schooling models. If I know Mo, I'd say he's been investigating potential business opportunities in what seems to be a growing market (sorry to let the cat out of the bag, Mo!):

> "There are a lot of different teaching systems. Another approach is student-centred approach, which is enquiry-based learning, which is good for children with ADHD, as they get to learn about

things that interest them. The students decide what they want to learn about.

They used to do that in America in forties, and then the war happened and they realised that Japan was better at technology that America, so one of their lobbying groups blamed it on the way they taught their students. So, they let go of the enquiry-based teaching, and they turned all of the schools into direct instruction teaching.

According to doctor Mo "a lot of people have started home schooling" their ADHD children. He doesn't necessarily think that it's a good thing, because he hasn't seen the evidence on either side, but as it's a different school model, he finds it very interesting as a potential improvement on the current system for ADHD'ers. "If the learning is fun enough, some kids with ADHD are going to be able to get so excited about learning that they may be able to get obsessed with and hyper-focus on the teacher and learning, and then do very well."

Challenges: Force, Punishment, Rebellion and Boredom

With 40% of children with ADHD developing oppositional defiant disorder, trying to force an ADHD'er to do something, may only create more resistance. Symptoms include chronic aggression, a tendency to argue, ignore requests and engage in intentionally annoying behaviour.

As an adult, Kat doesn't even like her GPS telling her what to do, let alone a teacher or manager. "I turn off the voice and prefer to just follow the map on the screen, so that I don't have to be told what to do!" She laughed. I laughed too, I was scared not to.[2]

Reframed from the ADHD'ers point of view, one of the most common traits of people with ADHD is the tendency to think for themselves, and resist being forced to do things that they don't enjoy, or that can't be logically explained as worthwhile. As adults, we are expected to think for ourselves, and it's a good thing. Children are expected to be obedient, and often unquestioningly so.

During childhood, being tenaciously independent can have a negative outcome, such as expulsion from school or problems with relationships at home. It is probably a biased point of view for me to hold, but for some interviewees, their schools and parents seemed determined to "break" their will rather than change their own approach and cater to their strengths. Perhaps this is unavoidable in a world that places value in academic strength across the board, rather than allowing early specialisation.

All of my subjects discuss how if a subject is fun or interesting, it makes them want to learn about it. But at school if something was boring and forced on them, it created resistance, defiance and worst of all, make them feel deficient in some way.

Alex explained that trying to force him to enjoy his school work simply didn't work. "If you don't know whether you like a subject or not, and you have people telling you to like it, it's not going to work. You won't do your homework and you're going to get in trouble."

It's a similar story for Kyle. "I couldn't abide by the school system, I couldn't play by the rules. I had to ask why." He questions schools that place more emphasis on children tucking their shirts in and following the rules than it does on their education:

> "Obviously, the school system doesn't want you to do that, the school system wants you to just say "yes sir, no sir" and do as you're **** told. It breeds a level of conformity. And I was never just that person."

At Kyle's school, punishment was preferable to exploring his disruptive behaviour or explaining rules reasonably- which only served to perpetuate the problem:

"I would be disruptive in school, and no teacher would ever ask "Why did you behave like that in class, Kyle?" I would get punished. And that punishment would perpetuate into more disruptive behaviour. Because you can't punish a kid for the way that they're feeling about something without ever asking them why, and expect that to be the answer. Expect them to say "okay, lesson learned, I'm going to be a good boy now," it does not work like that.

But actually, if one of my teachers had sat me down and tried to explain to me, on a human level, why I had to tuck my shirt in, or why I wasn't allowed to listen to music on my lunchbreak, or all of these things that I had an issue with, I would have been a different story at school. But punishment doesn't work with kids with ADHD. It generates more of a will to be disruptive, and to continue that behaviour that got you punished in the first place, it simply doesn't work."

After talking to my friends about their experiences, and weighing these up against the responsibilities of adults trying to teach them, I have lots of questions (unfortunately without any answers):

- *Adults are responsible for the safety of children in their charge, and for teaching them valuable life-lessons. But is questioning instructions or resisting doing things they don't enjoy always bad?*

- *Are oppositional children acting like adults before their time?*

- *Do some oppositional children potentially have in depth thought processes behind their behaviours? Are some of them actually standing up for a value, or insisting on knowing the reason for something, when they resist doing what they are told? If so, would listening to them and asking why, help to solve the problems?*

- *Would they behave differently if they understood the why's and wherefores?*

- *Is there a way to allow children to focus more on their natural passions, rather than expecting them to take an interest in the entire range of school subjects? Would this result in a better application of effort, rather than energy being poured into resistance?*

- *Does an enforced broad approach risk disengagement and drop-out, as opposed to thriving in a speciality approach? Or would allowing a focused or specialised approach earlier in school make impulsive kids vulnerable to bad teachers or particularly "boring" modules?*

- *Should children learn all subjects for so long, in case they "find passion" for them in the future, or in case they need them as a foundation for another subject?*

Unfortunately, I don't have any answers to these questions, but in the future, I intend on setting up a debate between my most rebellious ADHD superstars, such as Kyle, and high-ranking teachers within the school system, who may be able to answer their questions and potentially give the opposing point of view.

If you'd like to be added to the waiting list to be notified when this comes out you can email rachel.knight.books@gmail.com, and I'll be sure to let you know.

As frustrating as it may be for ADHD'ers in education and the adults trying to help (or hinder) them, I would presume the answers would be different for each individual. For now, the verdict from our superstars was clear, the system needs to change.

Challenges: Dropping out of School or University

It's important to realise that dropping out of education, or even finishing education that was never used, has not stopped our superstars from achieving their ultimate goals, and seems to be a common delay to their eventual success.

When Kyle started to question the relevance of school rules, he found himself locked in a disruptive cycle that spiralled out of control, and ended in his expulsion. "In my early years, I got kicked out of school before my GCSEs. I got in a lot of trouble, I was extremely disruptive," he told me.

> "It became this totally endlessly self-perpetuating thing that got worse and worse and deepened and deepened. The school system failed in so many ways."

Doctor Mo explained how the current system, leads to ADHD children disengaging and dropping out of school. He was in his fifth year of medical school, before anxiety surrounding his ADHD symptoms caught up with him, almost causing him to drop out:

> "I wasn't doing very well [at medical school], I did fine up until fourth year but in the fifth year the anxiety caught up with me, and one of the things people with ADHD struggle with is they're more sensitive to anxiety, they have bad coping mechanisms. So, I started to look into why this was happening to me, and why I couldn't focus, why I couldn't bring myself to go in to lectures. It was weird that I wasn't able to do that when everyone else could. Diagnosis for me was very important.

> When I found out I had ADHD, I read more about it and I realized I should pursue the positive aspects and try to make them work for me."

According to Mo, children and young adults with ADHD face the challenge of remaining engaged in education, because the system is built to cater for the majority of children, rather than those with a low boredom threshold:

> "The majority of kids are able to do well, you're forcing kids to learn science and maths and languages, and everything that's good for society. But there's a group who get so disengaged that they drop out or look for thrills elsewhere, get addicted to drugs etc. A lot of these kids have ADHD."

Mo believes that the danger lies with the ensuing boredom and impulsivity that can lead children and young adults to make careless mistakes, that then affect their lives as a whole:

> "Once something bad happens in your life, it's very easy to spiral. But people don't make the connection. But because you're impulsive, you may well end up doing something stupid eventually, if you don't have a passion to direct you towards something productive or positive."

This is exactly what happened to Alex, whose impulsivity and boredom with education led to expulsion from school and dropping out of university. "I got in loads of trouble at school. I don't know why," he told me, suddenly laughing and changing his mind after thinking about it "No, I do know why. Hahaha!" He explained how he had been doing well at a specialist school for dyslexics, which helped him. But when he got caught smoking he was suspended, and then was later expelled when he was caught with marijuana. Spending a year studying at university, he realised he didn't like the subject. "I couldn't do another two years. So, I went to work for my dad in London."

I can't help but wonder, if the education system had been more engaging for ADHD'ers, and if my interviewees had been able to follow their passions in school (including non-curriculum activities such as learning entrepreneurialism, how to network, survival skills, journalism, setting up a business or charity, investments etc.), would they have disengaged and dropped out?

It makes sense that a "drop-out stage" could be the riskiest part of a young ADHD'ers life. Feelings of confusion and guilt about why they can't fit into a system that everyone else fits into is understandable. They need support from their families, who may well be disappointed in them. Suddenly the pressure can be on to quickly find the "right" direction, as well as the motivation to "turn things around." Perhaps for some people, things spiral out of control, and they find that they never find their passion, and they never come to believe in themselves. *Are these the ADHD'ers that take the easy way out and end up in prison, or self-medicating on drugs and alcohol?*

It's not difficult to see how many people with ADHD could become focused on exciting pursuits such as socializing, drinking, doing drugs, gambling, or criminal activity, in the absence of something constructive. Particularly if they don't believe they could have success at anything else.

What about children that get into trouble at school, and don't have supportive or understanding parents? What about parents who are incapable of seeing the world through the eyes of someone who's "different" from them, are apathetic, involved in criminal behaviour themselves, or absent from their children's lives? An incident of "trouble" for children from households like these, could lead to very different outcomes.

Perhaps for people with ADHD, outcomes in life are particularly susceptible to what they are exposed to, and what fun activities come along to absorb their interest, particularly if they drop out of the system.

A Flexible Approach to Learning

Most interviewees struggled to make consistent effort at subjects that bored them or that they saw as having no tangible benefit. Not doing their homework or taking a cramming approach to exams seemed to work out for them, if allowed.

Kat explained that being given the flexibility to approach her schoolwork and career in her own way, both at home and at school, helped her maintain a positive outlook towards her own abilities: "So instead of studying the whole year I was just studying for the exams. My teachers were flexible enough to allow me to do any make up lessons."

> "I was one of those kids who was coasting most of the year and then when the exam time came was catching up at the end of the year and pulling my grades up. I was never able to just go at the same pace, do all of the boring things and focus on things the whole year. But I just did some make up tests and learn the material quickly. It was always easier to learn the things that I was interested in.

Learning for Kat loses its importance when she doesn't see any future use in learning about it, and this means she naturally resists putting effort into it:

> "When I see something as useless I find it very difficult to learn them. I hated history because the way they teach it in Poland was not about understanding politics (which would have been fascinating) they made us memorise dates, and number of troops, names of battles. It was so boring, I had no interest in that."

Kyle's view was much the same, but he poured far greater energy into resisting the "pointlessness" of learning subjects like trigonometry, landing himself in hot water for his views. For Kyle, the school system never broke his will, and he has since thrived by embracing his individuality.

In contrast, doctor Mo, with inattentive style ADHD rather than hyperactive or combined, was able to coast through school without a diagnosis, and catch up at the end of term.

> "I realized I'd never paid attention at school, and that I'd possibly paid attention for about 10% of the time across the whole school year.
>
> Nobody cared that I wasn't paying attention because I'd always do well at school. I'd go home two weeks before the exam and I'd cram everything. So, nobody cared, the teacher would look at me, I'd be

making a paper airplane, but I was never disruptive because I had the inattentive type."

Despite Ray hyper-focusing on what the teacher was saying in subjects he liked, he still couldn't make herself do his homework, and appreciated the fact that he didn't get into too much trouble for it.

It seemed from my interviews, children with ADHD seem to do better with a less rigid, more human approach to learning and discipline, that allows them to spend less time on things that bore them and focus on their passions and strengths.

How did ADHD affect family life?

Our families shape us a great deal, from our values to our social skills to our image of ourselves and our competence. Because children with ADHD can be difficult to manage, family relationships can often suffer. As a result of this, many people with ADHD suffer from self-esteem issues, partly because of their difficulties conforming with the expectations of those around them, but this is not necessarily so.

Doctor Mo explains:

> "It's very important to look at the aspect of how to deal with children with ADHD. It can seem like everything they do, they're doing it on purpose or vindictively, but that is almost never the case. So, it's

good to bear that in mind when you're dealing with them.

For example, if someone is not paying attention when you're talking, it's not because they think what you're saying is boring or they don't care about you, it's because they literally can't focus. And don't criticize them because they're very sensitive to criticism, most kids with ADHD, which can lead to a lot of personality disorders, anxiety or depression, in my opinion. Because they don't feel they're good enough, because they're not conforming."

Framing ADHD Correctly

Kyle demonstrates the point of view that ADHD is something to be proud of perfectly, highly recommending it to others, and unsure if he would have achieved so much without it. This is a viewpoint shared by Richard Branson (founder of Virgin) and Olympic gold-medallist Michael Phelps' mother. Kat also sees herself as *more* capable of getting things done than most people, something she is complimented on by others.

Doctor Mo explains that framing a diagnosis of ADHD in the right way, is very important so that it doesn't feel like a deficiency label.

"Without a diagnosis, you feel weird that everyone else can do all of these things except you. But if you have all of the knowledge, and someone tells you why you can't do things, not because you lack something compared with all of the other children who can do all of these mundane tasks, it's because your brain is wired in a way that is slightly different.

Explain to them that they'll be able to become an artist, an athlete, a business person. Show them the plus side of having all of these traits, because most kids can't see it yet, they're still so young. They get immersed in a world of repetitive, mundane responsibility, and the positives of ADHD sometimes come out later in life when you are able to pursue your passions."

Did family approaches to learning affect them?

Property developer Ray, described how his mum made learning competitive so that he became "that really annoying kid who had my hand up at every question."

"From a very young age she made us love learning. I don't know how. But she used to spend a lot of time with us when we were little so that we really enjoyed

> it when we got something right. We got a lot of praise. So, getting something right was really fun."

Kat's mum helped her with her schoolwork and made things more interesting:

> "She would put things into little games, which were brilliant. This is what helped me to really love some subjects. I hated the subjects she couldn't make interesting. She would put them in context, make them "dance" pretty much."

Kyle counts himself lucky that he had such an accepting and supportive mother. He was allowed a great deal of creative expression:

> "I can certainly vouch for the fact that my mum gave me a lot of freedom, and I'm a very confident and self-assured person these days. I don't know how much that has to do with it, but that's my experience."

According to doctor Mo, when it comes to learning, people with ADHD will find it difficult to absorb something that they don't like, whether or not they are pushed into it. "The best thing to do as a parent is to pick your battles and find something that your child will be interested in, and at least they can learn something." This coincides well with our previous insights that finding productive passions and areas of hyper-focus works well.

At home, doctor Mo's mother even went so far as to take "three weeks off work" to teach him English. For him, a deadline along with an incentive for a good performance worked well to encourage learning. He doesn't necessarily advocate this kind of incentive, but he can vouch it worked well for him.

> "She used different mechanisms, like paying me to read. She manipulated me into doing it, by cutting down my pocket money and gave it back to me through reading, so I got hustled in a way. We used to get extra money every quarter based on our grades.
>
> The best thing to do is to give yourself or your child an incentive. I didn't want to read a lot as a child, so my mother paid me for every book that I finished."

Challenges: Rebellion Against Parents

Resisting and rebelling against parents was common amongst interviewees who report being pressured into obeying. Alex, Veronica, Ray and doctor Mo all report resisting parental influence as a common occurrence.

Despite having a good relationship with his parents, doctor Mo recalls that he was extremely difficult for his parents to deal with, and gives a lot of credit to his mother for her resilience. "If you have a child with ADHD it's very easy to give up. But my mum persevered so much," he told me. According to doctor Mo he did everything wrong, and made his parents feel like they couldn't even get the basics right:

> "Everything in the parent's rulebook I did wrong. I never paid attention at school, I never tried to do my homework, I never stayed at home, I wouldn't sit on the couch for a second, I was just jumping around all over the place. All I wanted to do was play PlayStation, so my mum had to stop me from doing that. I wouldn't go to bed; my average bedtime would be about two am even as a ten-year-old. I made my parents feel like they were *** parents basically.

> To normal parents who knew basic things about parenting the only things you have to do as a parent is make sure your child goes to bed early, eat their food- which also I didn't do all the time- and not

spend hours in front of the TV. I wouldn't let my parents do any of them."

It's only my impression, but it seems like doctor Mo shoulders a lot of burden about for being so much trouble for his parents. He even referred to himself as a "crap human being" in reference to not enjoying a mundane task, once. I can't help but wonder if it's because lifelong expectations have been placed on him that are far from his natural tendencies.

Listening to him talk about six-year-old Mo running back and forth like a yo-yo, resisting all efforts to make him learn and sit quietly, I laugh, but really, I feel sad. Sometimes with Mo I'm sitting in a room with what feels like a frustrated horse. Trained to within an inch of its life, it wouldn't dare to buck the stables. I have visions that one day he'll slip his reigns, stampede the gates and rodeo the hell out of here. Perhaps the last I'll see of him is as he disappears up into the mountains, lassoing CEO's and making them sign up to his latest tech-start-up.

Despite it being very important for a child to learn, I also can't help but wonder if he should have been forced so strongly in a direction that made him so desperately uncomfortable. It'll never be known, whether some of his disengagement at school and frustration at home came from an environment that tried to force him to participate in quiet learning. Would matching his energy levels with learning games that were incredibly fun and boisterous have worked better? Would this have created less resistance and disruption from a child who didn't want to be broken into learning quietly? Would he still have that far away gaze in his eyes as he quietly feeds his hamsters humous? Who would I have in front of me if the little boy had not been forced to submit?

Rather than be openly disruptive like Mo and Kyle, Ray tended to withdraw into passivity, and refuse to take part in her family. "If the dice are loaded against me" he explained, "I will not take part in any form of conversation, debate or competition." The problem with parent-child relationships, according to Ray, is that the dice are always loaded. To him, when it comes to obedience "it's always been the merit of the argument that should win, not a title that is just given, which is what a parent is."

Like Kyle's attitude to questioning school rules that he saw as lacking any genuine reason, Ray couldn't stop questioning the reasoning behind his mother's obsession with tidying. "My mum would always ask me to tidy up. And I'd think, why?" His resistance to his mother's instructions spiralled more and more out of control, destroying a great deal of their relationship. He saw his mother as the driving force behind this degradation, which was something that he also couldn't understand.

As an adult, Ray can see that there are two sides to the story. Just as he wished that his mother had "been a bit more easy-going," his mother probably "wishes that I'd been a better son! Maybe she wins!" he jokes.

It seems like defiance can result in escalating gridlock that can't be solved by pushing. Perhaps defiance has its roots in a lack of understanding. If this is the case, maybe reasoning may work better, and if not, it may be a good idea to look at alternative methods, such as asking whether the rule could be relaxed, and if not, introducing an incentive to comply.

- *Should tenacity in ADHD children be broken or admired? Is there a middle ground?*

- *Does the rigor of the discipline and "structure" being imposed on a child relate to the level of rebellion?*

- *If I had been broken into a very calm and ordered household or school with high levels of discipline, would I have been "more broken" as an adult than if I had been broken into a creative and lively household or school? Would this then affect whether I could tap into my creativity, free will, tenacity and energy later in life? Would this affect my opinion of myself?*

Parents as inspiration

All of our ADHD'ers are self-employed or natural entrepreneurs, but some of them also saw people in their lives, such as parents, setting an entrepreneurial example for them to follow. This seemed to accelerate the process of them finding their own road to independence.

Alex's dad for example was "into investments and imports. So that really got me into it, that's what gave me the idea." Kat's stepfather, on the other hand was more of a deterrent to the self-employed way of life, as he didn't enjoy the long hours needed to run his business. Doctor Mo was inspired when his mother quit her job started her own business:

> "It was perfect. She had to be a mum and make money at the same time. So, she managed to start a business where she only had to work four months a year. And it made enough money for her to be completely independent, and put us through extra-curricular activities that cost a lot of money through the business. She still does that now. Works three or four months a year only."

The domino effect of leading by example was shown perfectly after he set up his ecommerce and nutrition businesses:

> "A lot of people around me started looking into business when I went into it. Because they realised that it's doable. If this person can do it, and we know him, then I can do it too."

Leading by example and creating an outside interest, whether entrepreneurially, charitably, artistically, socially, or in any other way, could be a powerful way to encourage an ADHD'er to explore their own natural gifts, and come up with some ideas of their own. It is also a much nicer alternative to forcing an activity on a child, as they get to watch a parent pursue an interest of their own. Thinking about it, it's also a pretty good litmus test for whether an activity is exciting enough to capture the excitement of an ADHD'er. If a parent doesn't get excited when they lead by example, a child is probably not going to be inspired by what they see.

Did their families worry?

Too much pressure from family to conform to a standard way of life, if their comfort-zone lies elsewhere, could leave an ADHD'er stuck in a life that doesn't feel right, or worse making reckless decisions. Impulsivity from ADHD can result in bad decision-making, drug taking, criminal activity, and a life that spirals out of control. But so too can over-caution prevent people with ADHD from fulfilling their potential.

Rather than dissuading an ADHD'er from taking a risky path (or one less travelled), finding situations from which they can make their own mistakes and learn how to mitigate their own risks, seems most applicable to these headstrong explorers. In reality, getting the balance right between encouragement and protection, seems like it could be a difficult challenge for parents.

At the risk of causing sexist controversy, doctor Mo discussed how the instinct to mother- and less so for fathers- in his opinion, can be extremely risk averse:

> "The problems mums will face is that they don't want their children to take risk. From a mother's point of view, of course she cares if their child has fun but their main concern is that they make it on their own, you become successful and you don't end up in trouble, in jail or on drugs.
>
> So, when you come up with an idea, they're going to think you're insane sometimes. Some mothers will just want you to do the boring things in life, and nothing else. A lot of mothers. A lot of mothers might make their children feel ashamed for being who they are.
>
> Sometimes if you have a good idea that sounds amazing, a lot of mothers won't want you to take that risk and potentially ruin your life if it fails. They

> want you to do the easy thing, make money and get a job. And be around. Mothers are often built to minimize risks through evolution, whereas often dads are the opposite. Mothers have to try and remember how they were, when they were children."

On the countering hand, doctor Mo is also aware of how risky decision making can lead to a downward trajectory in life.

Alex understands how worrying it can be for parents, concerned about the future of their ADHD children. "My mum worried about me so much," he told me. "They can get concerned about you and your direction in life." He faced considerable pressure to "fit in" with expectations both at home and at school.

Being honest, despite being incredibly impressed with what our ADHD superstars do for a living, if I was a parent I might feel as doctor Mo described. Rather than risking it all on working for themselves I might want them to have a nice easy job, with a regular income and stable lifestyle. But isn't that the point? It's not about what parents want, it's about helping children find and use their natural talents to live a life that's fulfilling to *them*.

If Alex has the ability to thrive with risk and uncertainty, then that's a gift, not a disadvantage. He's simply different from most people who would prefer to live their lives feeling secure, such as in a risk-free office job, which nearly bored him half to death. And if risky business makes him hyper-focus and gives him the lifestyle that he wants- then screw what anybody else thinks. It's taken him a while to find ways to improve the stability of his life, but as time has gone by his natural opportunistic tendencies have allowed him to capitalize on various income streams, avoid the ones that are too risky, and diversify his portfolio. All techniques that he has learnt for himself.

Kat told me a similar story, that like most mums, her mother "had the idea that it's best to have a career and make steady progress," until she realised, through independent reasoning, that it didn't make sense to her. All of our ADHD'ers have eventually found success on their own terms, which I discuss in the Career and Lifestyle section, next.

Career and Lifestyle Choices

Why do they lead unusual lives?

When it comes to independence, these ADHD'ers seem to have more in common with cats than with dogs, if my interviews are anything to go by. They're going to do their own thing eventually. Being free to decide their own path and being true to their own, unique reasoning, featured as important in all of my interviews.

I found this an incredibly interesting discovery. Some of the interviewees took long and winding roads to find a career that made them happy. Kat and Veronica tried to fit into a corporate career, Alex tried to fit into the office lifestyle, whilst Kyle happily did his own thing as a touring musician, before finding journalism as a professional pursuit.

Sadly, some people with ADHD seem to feel ashamed that they are unable to fit into a normal or regular life, rather than feeling proud to express their natural talents. Mo captured the irony of this well:

> "The last thing you want is someone with ADHD to feel like they're not good enough, while actually they can have some of the most amazing ideas that can change the world. It's very ironic for someone to be stuck in that situation."

Alex's epiphany moment happened while he was temping "answering the phone and finding bits of paper." I remember this period well, and at the time he talked about how life hadn't turned out like he had expected it to. "One day someone said to me 'Are you feeling okay? You're not looking well.' and I looked in the mirror, and my hair was all over the place, I looked absolutely dead. And I thought, I can't do this anymore."

Although he was very aware of how concerned his parents were about what he was doing with his life, and with a great deal of expectation on his shoulders, he realised "you need to do what you want to do. Trying to make other people happy, you're just going to be messed up."

Having known Alex for twenty years, and having watched him take many twists and turns, it's nice to see him doing his own thing:

> "I'd say I'm only just finding my path now, but before, I never really knew what I was going to do. But now, four things have fallen into place."

In terms of the risks involved in his day to day financial affairs, Alex has had to learn some lessons the hard way. He has made mistakes, he has lost thousands within minutes, and he's stayed awake for days on end watching the markets. He describes how when his gold and silver investments were doing well it would be "almost painful because it goes up and goes down. Its' very exciting." The excitement and worry at one point became too much for Alex, and again, he moderated his own behaviour to take control of the uncertainty in his own way:

> "I was addicted. When it went down it was too much. But you learn from that experience and decide not to do that *** any more. So, I got into stocks and shares. Now I'm into casino advertising. It's much more reliable, and brings in a pretty high income."

For Alex's investments to work, he has to be open to ideas and doing something different from the rest of the crowd. "You have to think differently, if you do the same as everyone else you're not going to make any money," he told me.

Kyle describes the "beautiful thing" about his life, is that he never knows what each new day will bring. This ex-touring-musician, ex-rowdy-journalist, ex-magazine founder and current agency co-owner, loves giving his best and letting the chips fall where they may:

> "I don't know if other people have this, but I thrive not knowing what's next. I thrive just living in the moment, doing the next project. And it always leads to something bigger, and more exciting. But I never know what's around the corner, and I love it."

Excitedly he tells me how opportunities "just keep arising." How, he could be living in New York in six months, has just bought a new apartment in central London, and has no idea which path he will take:

> "One of my biggest fears in life is being settled to a point where I could tell you what's going to happen in the next six months of my life. I have no idea

> what's going to happen in my life. And I love it. What a way to live life."

His journey only really began after he finished school, and was "in charge of his own education." As a child, he rejected being forced into a school system that didn't fit him, and as an adult, he still insists that his work environment allows him the freedom to express himself. "I have to work within a collaborative environment," he tells me, "I can't work within a totalitarian environment at all. That I would rebel against immediately, no matter what the circumstances."

Knowledge and education are hugely important to him, and he reads fervently on a wide range of subjects from philosophy, to sociology, classic literature and Russian literature from the eighteen-hundreds. "I've been able to apply a lot of this knowledge to my everyday life," he explains, rather than learning things for the sake of it, that he knows he will never use (although next time I see him, I'm going to ask how he plans to use Russian literature in his plans for world domination).

> "Since [school] I've gone on to do all sorts of things. Without any help from the school system. I've done it on my own accord, without any higher education at all."

Despite Kat's mother thinking that it is best to climb the career ladder steadily, when she thought about it, she couldn't see the sense in it, and decided to travel the world, running her own business while she did. She argues that having a job gives you an earning cap, whereas running your own businesses does not. So long as you're comfortable with risk and willing to work hard, she questioned why anyone would want a job over running their own business. She points out that so long as you are creative and adaptable in your approach, eventually your plans will work out:

> "You work and learn and get new skills. And so long as you keep learning you have to get to the point where it works. If you don't do new things you won't ever. But if you keep trying new things eventually it will.
>
> So, I can't understand why people would want a job over running their own business. And if you're in a job working 60 hours a week, there might be a time when a manager comes in, and completely screws it up for you, and you have to look for a new job, or the company goes under and you lose your stability. It just doesn't make any sense. It's better to be in charge of your own destiny. Even if for a few years it might be difficult, eventually you are going to get there."

Kat summarizes a commonly felt ADHD sentiment by adding simply, "I never did well with people telling me what to do."

Veronica also tried her hand at a corporate career, before thinking better of it, and going travelling rather than just "sitting in the box that I though was expected of me:"

> "I had a few years in a design studio in a marketing agency. But it was really, I just couldn't do it, going in every day, sitting with people. I get quite anxious. I didn't have any creative freedom, I had to do everything to budget and to deadlines and it was really stressful and boring."

For her, one of her biggest achievements is the traveling she did:

> "I always believed you work to live rather than the other way around, and experiencing life is about getting out into the world and seeing it."

Doctor Mo, no stranger to following his own entrepreneurial pursuits, as discussed in the next section, urges caution when making seemingly trivial decisions, to prevent ADHD'ers becoming a statistic, and reiterates the importance of applying the energy and hyper-focus of ADHD in the right direction:

> "Once something bad happens in your life, it's very easy to spiral. But people don't make the connection. But because you're impulsive, you may well end up doing something stupid eventually, if you don't have a passion to direct you towards something productive or positive."

Although some of our interviewees have experienced these downward turns, all of them have recovered. But as we know, some people are not so lucky. The over-representation of ADHD'ers in the prison and alcoholic populations demonstrate this well.

Mo suggests an approach that manages stress carefully:

> "You have to manage your stress very well. Because you don't realise your stress creeps up on you. Some people don't make the connection between a stressful job and extra drinking on the weekend. But really, they're self-medicating. And they have no insight.

> Insight is a very important word with ADHD and stress. Most people when they reach critical levels of anxiety and stress with no insight into how that's affecting their actions, and that's why they spiral out of control."

What made them start their own businesses?

This is a difficult question, but it seems like our superstars started their own businesses because their personalities are geared this way. These personality traits include the ADHD gifts already listed; a tendency towards independence, original thinking, bravery, the ability to hyper-focus and being energised around pursuits that excite them.

My hero and ex-boss, Liz - despite not having interviewed for this book- pioneered the entire patient-recruitment industry. The first agency of its kind, she spotted the opportunity to match people looking for new medical treatments with medical research projects. Whilst many have tried to copy, she remained ahead of the game for over twenty years. Recently, just before she retired, her agency was the first to partner with a big pharma client and Apple's 'ResearchKit,' a suite of technology apps that allow data to be collected remotely.

Like many of our ADHD'ers she has her fingers in multiple pies, such as property and web domain real-estate. Never one to sit still for long, I'm eager to see if she delves into a new arena, or if it's truly time for her to put her feet up.

For doctor Mo, entrepreneurialism comes naturally. "I found entrepreneurship before I knew I had ADHD. When I found out, it made sense, because they call it the entrepreneurial disease." He explains that his hyper-focus coupled with the ability to spot new trends and to overcome his fear of risk to stop him allows him to act on his ideas:

> "Because I can learn something so quickly, that makes me a good opportunist. So, if I see a part of this [medical] industry that's lagging or just emerging and not mature as a market, then I can jump in, learn a lot about it and start doing it. I identify trends, see opportunities, and go for them. Which I think is a strength for a lot of people with ADHD, that's what they do."

Kyle, Kat, Alex and Veronica all show similar attitudes, throwing around ideas whether by themselves or with people they know. Kat and Veronica, both stumbled into starting their own businesses, by following their passions of travelling, and finding ways to fund it through organizing trips and freelancing. From there, their businesses grew and gained momentum and direction, rather than starting with a plan.

Kyle on the other hand had a business idea and immediately quit his job to start working on it. He used bravery to his advantage (also referred to as impulsivity when described as an ADHD 'symptom'), and backed it up with abundant energy and drive to follow through on his exciting idea:

> "I handed in my notice for my job the next day. Put a business model together for this. We went out and started pitching for investment, and we got £50,000."

In his case, all of the traits of ADHD aligned well to contribute to his success.

Challenges: Expectations, Problems Fitting-In and Shame

Doctor Mo's late diagnosis means that he remembers being confused why "everyone else can do all of these things" except him. Interestingly, when I asked him about the challenges of ADHD, the first thing he mentioned was the expectations of people who sit at the opposite end of the spectrum. Apparently even the conversations go differently, "because you're almost on a different wavelength."

The expectations of people without any ADHD traits can be biased against ADHD'ers. In the workplace, colleagues- even ones who know about ADHD, put heavier emphasis on the negative aspects over the positive, which is an inherent human bias, according to doctor Mo:

> "So, you do the positive things that ADHD enables you to do, that other people aren't doing, because of your hyper-focus or your ability to get more work done because you have excess energy- and they'll say, "oh thanks for doing that, that's amazing." But people will tell you to get your shit together if you come in five minutes late. They don't want to take the positives and the negatives, they just want the positives. And its human nature to weigh the negatives things as more important that the positives, which is a cognitive bias."

Veronica told me that flexible workplaces are the best, where results are valued and arrival and departure times are flexible. She gets on best with colleagues who "who realize that an idea that changes the profitability of an entire business model, with data to back it up, can be more important than being a bit late for a meeting or forgetting to reply to an email on the same day. Some things affect profitability, and others don't."

According to literature, children with ADHD can struggle to make friends and can be outcasts in social situations. Doctor Mo has a theory that children with ADHD, can often have a lot empathy, and can be a "good sport" about ADHD symptoms and other things people "do to them." "Unfortunately," he says, "they don't always receive the same thing from everyone else:"

> "As the result of maybe alienation or intense feelings, kids with ADHD might respond by shutting down their feelings in order to manage them."

It can be very confusing not to know why other people seem to be able to spend time doing things you find intolerably boring, whilst at the same time you hold extraordinary abilities that other people do not. With these insights in mind, I've come up with an exercise to put you in the frame of mind of an ADHD'er who is questioning themselves. These questions compare the real expectations my interviewees have struggled with, with the activities they have subsequently taken in their *stride*.

Answer each of these honestly to yourself:

- Should Mo be overly concerned because he doesn't enjoy unpacking his shopping or cooking dinner for himself, or should he be happy that he saves lives, and starts successful businesses?

- Did Kat make a mistake when she quit her nine-to-five career to travel the world- doing all the things she ever dreamed of- and earning a living at the same time?

- Should Kyle be ashamed that he rebelled against the machine, or be proud that he built a career in journalism, founding his own magazine and digital content agency (preserving his unique creativity as he did so)?

- Do you think Alex should have stayed answering telephones and "filing bits of paper," or made the leap into trading silver, gold and oil from an apartment with a swimming pool, near the beach, in sunny Tenerife?

- Should Liz worry more over the thousands of unanswered emails, or should she be prouder that she's helped patients find lifesaving medical research projects? (Yes, I want Liz to answer my emails, but frankly she probably has a lot to do, and I shall quietly bide my time.)

- Should Veronica feel proud that she runs her own successful web-design agency, or worry about not fitting in well as an employee?

Despite being clearly obtuse with these questions, I think that they demonstrate how "bigger-picture-abilities" can sometimes be lost when we only place importance on small things that people at the opposite end of the ADHD spectrum value. After all, unpacking groceries promptly never saved a man's life (at least not in any way that I can think of).

References

1. D. Archer, Forbes; ADHD: The Entrepreneur's Superpower. 2014.

   https://www.forbes.com/sites/dalearcher/2014/05/14/adhd-the-entrepreneurs-superpower/#4a1f064159e9

2. D. Kreps, RollingStone.com; 15 Musicians who Run Business Empires. 2014. http://www.rollingstone.com/music/pictures/15-musicians-who-run-business-empires-20140915/justin-timberlake-20140915

3. K. Goodin, Parenting.com; Famous People with ADHD. http://www.parenting.com/gallery/famous-people-with-add-or-adhd?page=0

4. AdultingwithADHD.com; 18 Famous People With ADHD Who Happen to be Women. 2016.

   http://adultingwithadhd.com/18-famous-people-adhd/

5. S. Perrault Ph.D., Psychology Today; Seven Habits of Highly Successful Entrepreneurs with ADHD. 2009.
   https://www.psychologytoday.com/blog/entrepreneurs-adhd/200909/seven-habits-highly-successful-entrepreneurs-adhd

6. F. Levin, Alcohol & Drug Abuse: practical guidelines for the treatment of substance abusers with adult attention-deficit hyperactivity disorder. Psychiatric Services, August 1999.

Appendices

Example Games for ADHD Kids to Find their Gifts

Making learning fun was a key learning from our ADHD superstars. This was the deciding factor about whether they could focus on it or not. I've included two examples of fun learning games to engage and excite children with ADHD. If you'd like to be notified when my upcoming book '100 Fun Ideas to Harness ADHD' is released, email me at: rachel.knight.books@gmail.com

"Cramming Game"

As we know, forcing consistent learning on someone with ADHD can create resistance. Some of my friends found that a cramming approach to school work worked better for them than consistent learning. If a cramming approach seems to work well for your child, then you might consider understanding what factors are at play. Let's break it down to discover what's at the heart of cramming, and decide whether we can use it in our approach.

Essentially, a cramming approach to studying is a great deal of energy being expended in a short period of time, due to either fear of failure or an incentive to do well. There is a deadline that needs to be met, which creates a large amount of motivation and energy to learn. Cramming is also a novelty, and isn't happening consistently on a day to day basis.

I'm not suggesting that you use the "fear" motivation approach at all, which seems to be used very often in a disciplinary environment. The fun approach sounds much more in tune with what the superstars are advocating.

Using a "deadline and incentive" game, to recreate the influences that induce "cramming" for exams, has the potential to be wonderfully fun, when applied creatively. This might sound complicated, but it's not. A very simple model of this is a straight-forward treasure hunt. Solving clues to find toys or chocolate eggs is exactly the kind of activity that uses this approach in a fun way. The toys and eggs are the incentive, the other children looking are the deadline, as well as competition.

Adapting a treasure hunt into a "cramming" game:

- Use a clue-based treasure hunt, so that your child guesses where to hunt next.

- At each spot on the treasure hunt you hide a reward, and a sheet of paper, with a passage of text for them to study.

- A reward could be a chocolate egg, a marble, a token (representing points), a grape, a coin (this could be a fun way to give them their pocket money), depending on the age of the child.

- Give them 3 minutes to study a passage, and try to remember it all. Take the paper away and ask a question about what they read.

- To get the next clue, they must answer correctly, if they get it wrong, they get another question.

- If they get 3 questions wrong, they have 1 more minute to study the piece of paper.

- If the child can't read, the game can be made much simpler, with easier questions.

Adding excitement:

- Think like a computer game: Introduce changing time limits for studying up on the facts, bonuses (e.g. For 3 correct questions in a row they get an extra marble or egg), forfeits and penalties (e.g. Every time they get a question wrong they have to stand on one leg for 30 seconds. Or repeat a silly rhyme. Or eat a cold baked bean. Or be squirted with a water pistol....)

- Mum or dad might even be competing for the marbles or chocolate eggs. (You might pretend that you want your child to get the questions wrong, in order to get your sticky hands on their treasure. So, ask them the hardest questions first, to try and trip them up. And tell them what you're doing, and that you want their treasure for yourself. Compete with them.)

- Don't be afraid to do something outrageous with them. The point is to make the game engaging, fun and motivating. You might want to forget about hierarchy and rules for a while. You might introduce a rule that if they get 5 questions wrong in a row, they lose half the chocolate eggs they've collected.

- Keep the pay-offs something that's highly desirable. You could choose simple incentives like the person with the most points or eggs at the end of the game chooses their favourite meal or a piggy back from mum or dad. Or slightly self-deprecating incentives, such as the winner of the game getting to squirt mum or dad with a water pistol, or throw a bucket of cold water over them (if you have more than one child playing, they're all going to enjoy watching that).

- For older children, you could create a "town" or "world" in your house, garden or street, with a corresponding map. This might include historical landmarks, works of art, geographic regions, planets of the solar system, or even just colours and shapes. The choices are endless. Make sure that the questions you ask as clues all link back to the subject they are learning about!

Cooling down

- If you're worried about over-excitement, be prepared with a "cool down" activity at the end of the game, such as musical statues, a meditation exercise or a video to watch, to start calming them down.

- Consider filming the game, so that you can watch the video back together, giving them a chance cool down and also to shout out the answers to the questions. That way, your children get to repeat the questions and answers again in a fun way, and repetition is very important to learning.

Tips

- You don't need to go to great lengths preparing for the game. Simply photocopying pages from a text book for them to study and hiding them around the living room with a clue on the back would suffice.

- Think about the rules and incentives in advance, and explain them at the beginning. This makes things fair. If you don't explain to them at the start that every time they get a question wrong, you're going to eat one of their chocolate eggs, they may get a little upset when you do.

- Keep the goals, subjects and incentives in line with your child's current life and learning abilities. You might need to adapt the game to keep it fun. For example, one week your child might be very excited to play for fidget spinners, the next week fidget spinners could be incredibly uncool and uninteresting.

- Never make a child feel stupid for not knowing an answer to a question. You might ruin the game, and perhaps even put them off learning. If they keep getting the questions wrong give, consider giving them longer to study the text next time. If it's too difficult, consider making the text simpler or easier to read. Try and foster a feeling of success and confidence. If your game involves you directly competing with them, you might choose to jokingly "celebrate" when they get a question wrong because you're more interested in winning their chocolate eggs or marbles than you are in helping them learn. This will show them that the pressure is really off them, and they can relax. Also, it shows them that it's really down to them to learn for themselves this time.

- You can accumulate previously used fact sheets, and even make corresponding "question cards" over the course of a school year, so that by the end of the school year you have an enormous pile of relevant questions to re-use. This uses repetition to your child's advantage, but you might not get so many chocolate eggs for yourself.

- For older children, call the game a "mission," challenge, or orienteering, something more adult than a treasure hunt.

- You can easily use an egg timer from a board game to time the cramming periods.
- The key here is fun, something they will want to play again. Get creative with your "cramming" games, forget that you're mum or dad for a while, and enjoy yourself as well.

Entrepreneurial Game

There are hundreds of ways you can encourage an ADHD child to be inventive, creative and persuasive, that will all benefit their entrepreneurial abilities as adults.

A very easy entrepreneurial game, focusing on the art of persuasion, might be to give your child a simple item like a pair of socks, and ask them to tell you why you should buy it, listing all of the positive qualities. If they can make you agree to buying them, they get a reward of some kind.

To make it more of a two-way exchange or debate, you could ask them to try and convince you to exchange the socks in their hands, with the pair you are currently wearing. Why should you go to all of the effort to take off your socks for their pair? Make it harder for them by giving them an old pair with holes in them, or a big woolly pair even though it's the middle of summer. If it's too difficult for them, make sure that the pair they are holding are much nicer (and fresher?) than the pair you have on. You can help them if needed by hinting at the more obvious benefits to the exchange.

Tip

- Don't expect a child to be a sales genius without some practice, perhaps make it relatively easy for your child to persuade you the first time your play this game. You can become more of a challenging customer over time.

- See where you can take the game, perhaps you might get them to start haggling for increased pocket money, if they promise to provide additional washing up services, or they get an extra snack if they can convince you of the nutritional benefits.

- If their improved persuasive skills spill over into the rest of your relationship, consider whether this is good or bad for *them*, even if you don't want to spend more time discussing your reasoning for rules. Persuasive skills are important and seem to come naturally to some people with ADHD. Whilst this can be inconvenient for disciplinary figures like parents during childhood, persuasive skills as an adult are hugely important to success. Try not to squash them in an attempt to maintain control, as this can lead to frustration and rebellion. A suitable outlet such as a game like this, can help to develop persuasive skills, so that children don't think of them as inherently "wrong," whilst also giving them an arena.

ABOUT THE AUTHOR

Rachel Knight uses her years of experience travelling the world, working in medical communications and her scientific background to investigate her own burning questions, assessing the evidence as she goes. She tries to strike the right balance between anecdotal evidence and published research studies, for an engaging, 'human' read, that's informative and based on known-facts.

With a Bachelor's degree in astrophysics, Master's degree in clinical research, and human experiences gained from living in five countries, she uses her broad knowledge base on a range of human and scientific subjects to fuel her questioning mind.

BOOKS BY RACHEL KNIGHT

Super ADHD: ADHD Hope and Help from Real, Successful People with ADHD

Anti-Aging Skincare: Does it Really Work? Proven ways to appear younger and how to determine what works, from an expert in clinical research

Diabetes and Foot Care for Patients: Essential tips to salvage your feet

Bladder Cancer for Patients and Families: Guidance, Patient Experiences and Practical Resources

Colon Cancer 101 for Patients: Empowered in our Fight against Bowel Cancer

Sign up to the reading list…

If you enjoyed this book, found it useful or otherwise then I'd really appreciate it if you would post a short review. I do read all the reviews personally so that I can continually write what people are wanting.

Sign up to my reading list at rachel.knight.books@gmail.com

Thanks for your support!

Printed in Great Britain
by Amazon